Green Bay Packers IQ:
The Ultimate Test of True Fandom

JOEL KATTE

This title is part of the IQ Sports History / Trivia Series, which is a
trademark owned by Black Mesa Publishing, LLC.

Cataloging-in-Publication Data is available from the Library of Congress.
ISBN: 978-0-9883648-7-5

First edition, first printing.

Cover artwork courtesy of Jason Prigge.
Back cover photo courtesy Susan Grayson. Special thanks to Marcie Mott.
Cover design by Holly Walden Ross.

Black Mesa Publishing, LLC
Florida

admin@blackmesabooks.com
www.blackmesabooks.com

DEDICATION

I dedicate this book to my wife Dawn, who yells at the television during Packers games with more passion than any other fan I have ever met. Her commitment to helping the coaching staff lead her team to victory is inspiring!

BLACK MESA IQ TITLES

CONTENTS

"I firmly believe that any man's finest hours—his greatest fulfillment of all that he holds dear—is that moment when he has worked his heart out in good cause and lies exhausted on the field of battle—victorious."

— *Vince Lombardi*

INTRODUCTION

The most successful football franchise of all-time was born in Green Bay, Wisconsin. The Green Bay Packers, the third oldest team in professional football, have won more championships than any other team. Although only about 100,000 people live in Green Bay, millions of Packers fans around the country and world root for this iconic team. Their green and gold merchandise is among the NFL's best sellers every year. If fans want to buy season tickets, they will be added to the waiting list of over 100,000 people in front of them. Many fans include their waiting list numbers in their wills and some have had to include their place on this list in divorce settlements. With millions of fans and such a rich tradition, the Green Bay Packers will be bringing football championships to "Titletown" for many generations to come.

Think you know Packers history? Think again. *Green Bay Packers IQ: The Ultimate Test of True Fandom* will test the most hardcore Packers fans. Regardless of your performance, go back and reread each chapter and memorize every fun, fascinating Packers fact to impress your friends and families at your next Packers party or tailgate outing. If you are fortunate enough to attend a game at Lambeau Field, after reading this book, your "cheesehead" will be filled with important Packers memories and knowledge to share with the fans of all ages sitting with you on the frigid cold aluminum bleachers. When you can answer 90% or more of the book's 350 questions, you have achieved ultimate fan status.

"Football is a great deal like life in that it teaches that work, sacrifice, perseverance, competitive drive, selflessness and respect for authority is the price that each and every one of us must pay to achieve any goal that is worthwhile."

— *Vince Lombardi*

1 THROUGH THE YEARS

Starting with the "Iron Man" era all the way through the 2012 season, the first 190 questions are likely to be as tough as the gritty men who played this great game without any helmets. If you make it through with only a few injuries and fumbles, you will be in good shape for a glorious Super Bowl finish!

THE "IRON MAN" ERA

Question 1: The Green Bay Packers were founded in the editorial room of the *Green Bay Press-Gazette*. The meeting was called by Curly Lambeau and George Calhoun. In what year was this great American franchise formed?
   a) 1909
   b) 1919
   c) 1920
   d) 1921

Question 2: When the Packers played their first game, the league was not called the NFL. What was the name of the league?

Question 3: When the Green Bay Packers and Chicago Bears rivalry started, what were the Bears known as?
   a) Wildcats

b) Bearcats
c) Staleys
d) Ditkas

Question 4: Andrew B. Turnbull was the Packers first what?
a) Quarterback
b) Punter
c) President
d) Coach

Question 5: How many regular season games did it take before the Packers beat the Chicago Bears?
a) Two
b) Three
c) Four
d) Five

Question 6: The Packers first played in City Stadium. What was its initial capacity?
a) 6,000
b) 12,000
c) 20,000
d) 26,000

Question 7: J.E. Clair of Acme Packing Company first owned the Packers franchise, but he turned it over to the league in 1922 after the team was disciplined for not obeying league rules. The franchise was purchased back for $250. How much of that did general manager and coach Curly Lambeau pay?
a) 50
b) 100
c) 150
d) 250

Question 8: In 1922, the Packers endured bad weather and poor attendance, so a public non-profit corporation was set up to save the team. How much money was raised?
a) $1,000

b) $2,500
c) $10,000
d) $25,000

Question 9: In 1927, the Packers stunned critics when they beat what "Big Town" franchise 13-0?

Question 10: In 1929, the Packers win their first NFL title. What was their final record?

ANSWER KEY

Question 1: B. 1919

Question 2: American Professional Football Association

Question 3: C. Staleys

Question 4: C. President

Question 5: C. 4

Question 6: A. 6,000

Question 7: A. $50

Question 8: B. $2,500

Question 9: New York Yankees (No, it was not the same New York Yankees featuring Babe Ruth and the Bronx Bombers.)

Question 10: 12-0-1

Keep a running tally of your correct answers!

Number correct: ___ / 10

Overall correct: ___ / 10

THE THIRTIES

Question 11: The Packers won their second NFL title with a 10-3-1 record. What year was this?
 a) 1930
 b) 1932
 c) 1933
 d) 1934

Question 12: True or False: The Packers won three consecutive NFL titles.

Question 13: In 1932, the Packers impressive winning streak was snapped after how many consecutive wins?
 a) 12
 b) 14
 c) 18
 d) 22

Question 14: In 1932, the Packers posted an impressive 10-3-1 record; however, the Chicago Bears won the NFL title that year. What was the Bears record?
 a) 11-2-1
 b) 10-2-2
 c) 8-4-2
 d) 7-1-6

Question 15: What Packers legend from Alabama became one of the best receivers of all-time?

Question 16: What incident in 1934 almost caused the Packers to fold?

Question 17: In 1936, the first NFL draft was held. Whom did the Packers select as their first ever number one draft choice?
 a) B. Johnny Blood McNally
 b) T. Cal Hubbard
 c) Russ Letlow
 d) Tony Mandrich

e) Mike Michalske

Question 18: In 1936, the Packers won their fourth NFL title. This was the first title under the playoff system. What team did the Packers defeat 21-6 to win this title?

Question 19: Where was the 1936 title game played?

Question 20: In 1938, the Packers reached the title game but lost 23-17. What franchise that still exists today won the 1938 NFL title?

Question 21: The Packers won the 1939 NFL title game 27-0. Where was this game played?
   a) Green Bay
   b) New York
   c) Chicago
   d) Milwaukee

ANSWER KEY

Question 11: A. 1930

Question 12: True

Question 13: D. 22 consecutive wins

Question 14: D. 7-1-6 (Yes, six tie games!)

Question 15: Don Hutson

Question 16: A fan fell from the stands at the old City Stadium. The fan sued and was awarded $5,000. After the insurance company went out of business, the Packers went into receivership and eventually were saved when local Green Bay business owners raised $15,000.

Question 17: Russ Letlow from the University of San Francisco

Question 18: Boston Redskins

Question 19: New York's Polo Grounds

Question 20: New York Giants

Question 21: D. Milwaukee

Keep a running tally of your correct answers!

Number correct: ___ / 11

Overall correct: ___ / 21

THE FORTIES

Question 22: The Packers and the Bears tied for the 1941 Western Division title. Who won the playoff game 33-14?

Question 23: 1n 1944, the Packers defeated the New York Giants 14-7 at the Polo Grounds to win their sixth NFL title. Name the Packer who scored both touchdowns.

Question 24: In 1945, Don Hutson set the all-time single quarter scoring record with 29 points, helping the Packers beat Detroit 57-21 in Milwaukee. How did he score the 29 points?

Question 25: In 1949, the Packers again faced financial woes, but they played a Thanksgiving intra-squad game at old City Stadium and raised funds. How much money did they raise?
- a) $25,000
- b) $35,000
- c) $50,000
- d) $60,000

ANSWER KEY

Question 22: Bears

Question 23: Ted Fritsch

Question 24: Don Hutson scored 29 points in one quarter by catching four touchdown passes and kicking five extra points.

Question 25: C. $25,000

Keep a running tally of your correct answers!

Number correct: ___ / 4

Overall correct: ___ / 25

THE FIFTIES

Question 26: In 1950, Curly Lambeau resigned to become vice president and coach of what team?
   a) New York Giants
   b) Boston Redskins
   c) Chicago Cardinals
   d) Houston Oilers

Question 27: In 1950, the Packers appeared to be in good financial standing when their stock drive netted how much money?
   a) $105,000
   b) $112,000
   c) $118,000
   d) $124,000

Question 28: In 1953, the Packers played in what new stadium on September 27?

Question 29: In 1953, Gene Ronzani resigned as coach. Name the two co-coaches who took over.

Question 30: The "New" Packers introduced new uniforms featuring what new color?

Question 31: Name the former Marquette University coach who became the Packers coach in 1954.

Question 32: In what year was construction completed on City Stadium just in time for an Opening Day 21-17 victory over the Chicago Bears?
   a) 1955
   b) 1956
   c) 1957
   d) 1958

Question 33: The Packers' 1956 4-8 record was actually better than their 1957 record. What was their 1957 record?

a) 4-7-1
b) 3-9
c) 2-10
d) 1-11

Question 34: Assistant coach Ray "Scooter" McLean took over as head coach in 1958 but resigned after the Packers worst year in franchise history. What was the Packers record under McLean?

Question 35: Iconic coach Vince Lombardi was named the Packers head coach and general manager in February 1959. Lombardi was the offensive assistant coach for what team before coming to Green Bay?

a) New York Giants
b) New York Jets
c) Buffalo Bills
d) University of Notre Dame

Question 36: In his first season with the Packers, coach Vince Lombardi helped the Packers post a winning record of 7-5. This was the Packers first winning record in how many years?

a) 7
b) 9
c) 11
d) 12

ANSWER KEY

Question 26: C. Chicago Cardinals

Question 27: C. $118,000

Question 28: Milwaukee County Stadium

Question 29: Hugh Devore and Ray "Scooter" Mclean

Question 30: Green

Question 31: Lisle Blackbourn

Question 32: C. 1957

Question 33: B. 3-9

Question 34: 1-10-1

Question 35: A. New York Giants

Question 36: D. 12 years

Keep a running tally of your correct answers!

Number correct: ___ / 11

Overall correct: ___ / 36

THE SIXTIES

Question 37: In 1960, the Packers won the Western Division title for the first time since what year?
- a) 1940
- b) 1942
- c) 1944
- d) 1946

Question 38: The Packers lost the 1960 NFL title game 17-13 to what team?
- a) Giants
- b) Jets
- c) Eagles
- d) Redskins

Question 39: Name the Packers legend who scored an NFL record 176 points in 1960.

Question 40: The record of 176 points scored in a single season stood until what year?
- a) 1986
- b) 1991
- c) 2003
- d) 2006

Question 41: In 1961, the Packers routed the New York Giants for their seventh NFL championship. What was the final score?

Question 42: What was significant about where the Packers 1961 title game was played?

Question 43: In 1962, the Packers again beat the Giants 16-7 in the NFL title game to win their second straight championship. Where was this game played?

Question 44: In 1965, Packers' founder and first coach E.L. "Curly"

Lambeau passed away on June 1. City Stadium was renamed Lambeau Field on September 11. How old was Lambeau when he passed away?
 a) 61
 b) 64
 c) 67
 d) 71

Question 45: What was significant about the Packers 13-10 win over the Baltimore Colts in the 1965 Western Conference playoff game?

Question 46: Who kicked the game winning 25-yard field goal in the 1965 13-10 Western Conference win over the Colts?

Question 47: In 1967, the Packers won the first "Super Bowl" when they defeated the AFL's Chiefs in Los Angeles. What was the final score?
 a) 24-17
 b) 35-10
 c) 17-10
 d) 28-17

Question 48: In 1967, the Packers beat the Dallas Cowboys 21-17 to win their third consecutive NFL title. What was the nickname given to this game? HINT: The temperature was 13 degrees below zero.

Question 49: Who scored the last-minute 1-yard touchdown to beat the Cowboys in this historic game?

Question 50: In 1968, the Packers won the second ever "Super Bowl" with a 33-14 win in Miami. Who did they beat to secure another NFL title?
 a) Oakland Raiders
 b) Kansas City Chiefs
 c) New York Giants
 d) Miami Dolphins

Question 51: Vince Lombardi resigned as Packers coach after the 1968 season. He remained in Green Bay as the Packers general manager. However, in 1969 he resigned his role as general manager to become part-owner, executive vice-president, and head coach of what NFL team?
 a) Oakland Raiders

b) Kansas City Chiefs
c) Washington Redskins
d) New York Jets

Question 52: Name the Packers head coach who replaced Vince Lombardi.

ANSWER KEY

Question 37: C. 1944

Question 38: C. Eagles

Question 39: Paul Hornung

Question 40: D. 2006 LaDanian Tomlinson broke the record with his 30th touchdown of the season.

Question 41: 37-0

Question 42: This was the first title game played in Green Bay.

Question 43: New York's Yankee Stadium

Question 44: C. 67

Question 45: The 13-10 win was the first Packers game in overtime in franchise history.

Question 46: Don Chandler

Question 47: B. 35-10

Question 48: "Ice Bowl"

Question 49: Bart Starr scored a last-minute 1-yard touchdown on a quarterback sneak.

Question 50: A. Oakland Raiders

Question 51: C. Washington Redskins

Question 52: Phil Bengston

Keep a running tally of your correct answers!

Number correct: ___ / 16

Overall correct: ___ / 52

THE SEVENTIES

Question 53: Packers legend Vince Lombardi passed away on September 3, 1970. How old was he?
a) 54
b) 57
c) 59
d) 61

Question 54: After coach Bengston resigned in 1970, this coach from the University of Missouri became the Packers head coach and general manager in 1971.

Question 55: In 1972, the Packers finished 10-4 and won the division title. When was the last time they had won their division?
a) 1967
b) 1968
c) 1969
d) 1970

Question 56: Despite winning their divisional title in 1972, the Packers title hopes ended when they lost 16-3 in the playoffs. What team did the Packers lose to?
a) Kansas City Chiefs
b) Denver Broncos
c) Washington Redskins
d) Miami Dolphins

Question 57: Dan Devine resigned as head coach in 1974. What was his combined record for the 1973 and 1974 seasons?
a) 11-17
b) 14-14
c) 11-15-2
d) 12-15-1

Question 58: Bart Starr was named the Packers head coach and general manager in 1974 but unfortunately he was never able to replicate the same success he'd had on the field as a player while serving in this new capacity. Starr never won an NFL title coaching, but he had no problem winning as QB. How many NFL titles did he win as quarterback for the Packers?

a) 3
b) 4
c) 5
d) 6

ANSWER KEY

Question 53: B. 57

Question 54: Dan Devine

Question 55: A. 1967

Question 56: C. Redskins

Question 57: C. 11-15-2

Question 58: C. Five titles

Keep a running tally of your correct answers!

Number correct: ___ / 6

Overall correct: ___ / 58

THE EIGHTIES

Question 59: Judge Robert J. Parins was elected Packers President in 1982. He replaced Dominic Olejniczak. What was significant about Parins taking over?

Question 60: In what year did Bart Starr stop being the Packers head coach?
  a) 1981
  b) 1982
  c) 1983
  d) 1984

Question 61: What Packers legend signed a five-year head coaching contract in 1984?

Question 62: In 1985, the Packers added 72 private boxes at Lambeau Field bringing its capacity up to what?
  a) 52,357
  b) 56,926
  c) 58,782
  d) 60,711

Question 63: What year did the Packers generate their first $2,000,000 annual profit?
  a) 1986
  b) 1987
  c) 1988
  d) 1989

Question 64: In 1986, the Packers created the Green Bay Packers Foundation to do what?

Question 65: In 1988, coach Forrest Gregg resigned to become the coach at his alma mater. What school did he attend and later become head coach at?
  a) Notre Dame
  b) University of Mississippi

c) Southern Methodist University
d) University of Florida

Question 66: Name the Cleveland Browns offensive coordinator who signed a five-year contract to be Green Bay's next head coach?

Question 67: After Judge Parins retired as president, who was elected to be the next president and CEO of Packer Corporation?

Question 68: In 1989, the Packers released plans to create 1,920 club seats. Where did they place these seats?
a) North end zone
b) South end zone
c) East 50 yard line
d) West 50 yard line

Question 69: In addition to the addition of the club seats, the Packers added 36 additional boxes. What was the estimate of the total cost of the projects?
a) $6,500,000
b) $7,300,000
c) $7,800,000
d) $8,200,000

ANSWER KEY

Question 59: Parins became the Packers' first full-time CEO in franchise history.

Question 60: 1983

Question 61: Forrest Gregg

Question 62: B. 56,926

Question 63: C. 1986 (One year later the Packers reported over $3,000,000 in profits.)

Question 64: To make a commitment to contributing to charities.

Question 65: C. Southern Methodist University

Question 66: Lindy Infante

Question 67: Bob Harlan

Question 68: B. South end zone

Question 69: D. $8,200,000

Keep a running tally of your correct answers!

Number correct: ___ / 11

Overall correct: ___ / 69

THE NINETIES

Question 70: The Packers added two years to Lindy Infante's contract extending his tenure through what year?
- a) 1991
- b) 1992
- c) 1993
- d) 1994

Question 71: In 1991, former Pro Bowl safety Michael R. Reinfeldt and Los Angeles Raiders executive became the Green Bay Packers first what?

Question 72: Where do the Packers place the names of their Hall of Famers?

Question 73: In 1991, Ron Wolf was named executive vice president and general manager by Bob Harlan. Wolf was given full control of the Packers operation. Wolf came from what organization where he was director of player personnel?
- a) Buffalo Bills
- b) New York Jets
- c) New York Giants
- d) New England Patriots

Question 74: Wolf named Mike Holmgren the 11th Packers head coach. What team did Holmgren come from where he served as offensive coordinator?
- a) Los Angeles Raiders
- b) San Francisco 49ers
- c) Seattle Seahawks
- d) Denver Broncos

Question 75: Wolf dealt his first round draft pick in order to secure quarterback prodigy Brett Favre from what team?
- a) Atlanta Falcons
- b) New Orleans Saints
- c) Tampa Bay Buccaneers

d) Kansas City Chiefs

Question 76: In 1992, Mike Holmgren became only the third coach in franchise history to do what?

Question 77: Name the future Hall of Famer who the Packers signed as a free agent in 1993.

Question 78: In 1993, this Packer invented the "Lambeau Leap" when the Packers defeated the Raiders 28-0 despite the minus 22 degrees wind chill temperature.

Question 79: In 1993, the Packers clinched a playoff berth for the first time since what year?
   a) 1980
   b) 1982
   c) 1985
   d) 1987

Question 80: What team did the Packers defeat 28-24 in the 1994 wild-card playoff?
   a) Atlanta Falcons
   b) New Orleans Saints
   c) Tampa Bay Buccaneers
   d) Detroit Lions

Question 81: In July of 1994, the Packers dedicated their new $4.67 million indoor practice facility. What did they name the facility?

Question 82: The Packers played their last game at Milwaukee County Stadium on December 18, 1994. They beat the Atlanta Falcons 21-17. How many years had the Packers played in Milwaukee?
   a) 47
   b) 56
   c) 62
   d) 67

Question 83: The Packers finished the 1994 season with a 9-7 record and earned their second consecutive playoff berth. It was also their third consecutive winning season. When was the last time the Packers recorded three consecutive winning seasons?

 a) 1961-1963
 b) 1965-1967
 c) 1977-1979
 d) 1983-1985

Question 84: What Packers legend and record holder was released in 1995?

Question 85: When the Packers defeated the Pittsburgh Steelers in the final 1995 regular season game, they clinched their first NFC Central Division Championship since what year?

 a) 1972
 b) 1977
 c) 1982
 d) 1983

Question 86: In the first round of the 1995 playoffs, the Packers beat the Atlanta Falcons 37-20 at Lambeau Field. With the win, the Packers remained perfect at home during playoff games. How many home playoff games in a row had they won?

 a) 7
 b) 9
 c) 10
 d) 12

Question 87: The Packers knocked off the defending Super Bowl Champion San Francisco 49ers in 3Com Park on January 6, 1996. What was the score?

 a) 13-6
 b) 17-10
 c) 21-17
 d) 27-17

Question 88: In 1996, the Packers won their second consecutive NFC Central Division Championship when they trounced this team 41-6.

Question 89: The Packers went on to beat the San Francisco 49ers and Carolina Panthers to advance to the Super Bowl for the first time since

what year?
  a) 1965
  b) 1966
  c) 1967
  d) 1968

Question 90: Who did the Packers beat 35-21 in Super Bowl XXXI?

Question 91: Where was Super Bowl XXXI played?

Question 92: The Packers won another "title" with a victorious showing in Super Bowl XXXI … how many NFL titles did this bring to "Titletown"?
  a) 10
  b) 11
  c) 12
  d) 13

Question 93: The Super Bowl Champion Packers returned to Green Bay and paraded through town for three hours in front of adoring fans who endured the 0 to 10 degrees below zero temperatures. How many fans were estimated to see the Packers parade?
  a) 75,000
  b) 100,000
  c) 150,000
  d) 200,000

Question 94: Packers wide receiver legend Don Hutson died on June 26, 1997. How old was he when he passed away?
  a) 81
  b) 84
  c) 87
  d) 90

Question 95: The Packers two practice fields were named after what two Hall of Famers?

Question 96: In 1997, Packers Quarterback Brett Favre signed a contract that at the time made him the highest paid player in NFL history. How many years did he sign the contract for?

a) 5
b) 6
c) 7
d) 9

Question 97: In Ashwaubenon, Wisconsin, Gross Avenue, which intersects Lombardi Avenue, was renamed what?

Question 98: In 1997, Packers' shareholders agreed to offer 400,000 shares at $200 per share. This was the first time additional Packers stock was issued since what year?
a) 1940
b) 1950
c) 1960
d) 1970

Question 99: After the announcement, the Packers received how many phone calls concerning the stock offering?
a) 5,500
b) 15,000
c) 35,000
d) 55,000

Question 100: In 1997, the Packers clinched their franchise-record fifth consecutive postseason berth with a 27-11 victory over this team.
a) Minnesota Vikings
b) Chicago Bears
c) Detroit Lions
d) Tampa Bay Buccaneers

Question 101: The Packers then beat the Tampa Bay Buccaneers 17-6 to win their third straight NFC Central Division title. What else did this win mean for the Packers?

Question 102: In 1998, after beating the Tampa Bay Buccaneers in the divisional playoff round and then beating the San Francisco 49ers in the NFC championship game, the Packers advanced to the Super Bowl for the second year in a row. To whom did they lose 31-24 in Super Bowl XXXII after their last minute drive fell short?

Question 103: Super Bowl XXXII set a record for television viewers. The game was televised in 147 countries. How many people tuned in to watch the game?
a) 400 million
b) 600 million
c) 800 million
d) 1 billion

Question 104: How many fans welcomed the Packers back to Lambeau Field after their Super Bowl defeat?
a) 15,000
b) 25,000
c) 45,000
d) 75,000

Question 105: On March 8, 1998, Hall of Fame linebacker and fan-favorite Ray Nitschke died in Florida. How old was he when he passed away?
a) 61
b) 67
c) 70
d) 73

Question 106: In 1998, the Packers announced that they added 106,000 new shareholders. How much money did these shareholders add to the Packers franchise?
a) $12 million
b) $15 million
c) $20 million
d) $24 million

Question 107: In 1998, the Packers traveled overseas to play for the first time in franchise history. They defeated the Kansas City Chiefs 27-24 in overtime. Where was this game held?

Question 108: On September 25, 1998, the Packers extended their home winning streak to break the franchise record and tie for the second longest home winning streak in NFL history. How many games in a row did they win at Lambeau Field?

a) 20
b) 23
c) 25
d) 27

Question 109: The home field winning streak ended after which team beat the Packers on a rainy Monday night?

a) Minnesota Vikings
b) Chicago Bears
c) Detroit Lions
d) Oakland Raiders

Question 110: The Packers clinched another playoff berth in 1998, setting a franchise record for the most consecutive playoff appearances. How many years in a row were the Packers bound for the playoffs?

a) 5
b) 6
c) 7
d) 8

Question 111: The Packers were not destined for a third consecutive Super Bowl. After Brett Favre led the Packers to an 89-yard touchdown drive to take a 27-23 lead over the San Francisco 49ers, the 49ers scored in the final second to win 30-27. How many seconds were left when the 49ers scored their winning touchdown?

a) 17
b) 13
c) 8
d) 3

Question 112: Coach Mike Holmgren resigned from the Packers to do what?

Question 113: What former Packers' defensive coordinator and Eagles head coach replaced Holmgren?

Question 114: Fan-favorite Reggie White retired on February 15, 1999. How many years did this eventual Hall of Famer earn a Pro Bowl selection?

    a) 10

    b) 11

    c) 12

    d) 13

Question 115: When White's Jersey was retired at halftime of a game against Tampa Bay on October 10, 1999, the legend said, "I have been honored and privileged to have been a Packer, and I will always be a Packer." What years did this beloved player wear Packer green and gold?

Question 116: *Sports Illustrated* rated Lambeau Field as one of the top 20 best places in the world to view a sporting event. It was the only NFL stadium to crack the top 20. What ranking did the historic field receive?

    a) 4th

    b) 8th

    c) 11th

    d) 16th

Question 117: The largest crowd to view a Packers game in Wisconsin was 78,184. Where did all these fans watch the Packers beat the Denver Broncos on August 23, 1999?

ANSWER KEY

Question 70: D. 1994

Question 71: Chief Financial Officer

Question 72: On the walls of Lambeau Field's private boxes with the team's championship years in the south end zone.

Question 73: B. New York Jets

Question 74: B. San Francisco 49ers

Question 75: A. Atlanta Falcons

Question 76: He finished his first season as head coach with a winning record. They finished 9-7.

Question 77: Reggie White

Question 78: LeRoy Butler

Question 79: B. 1982

Question 80: D. Detroit Lions

Question 81: The Don Hutson Center

Question 82: C. 62 years

Question 83: B. 1965-1967

Question 84: Sterling Sharp

Question 85: A. 1972

Question 86: B. 9

Question 87: D. 27-17

Question 88: Denver Broncos

Question 89: C. 1967

Question 90: New England Patriots

Question 91: Louisiana Superdome in New Orleans

Question 92: C. 12

Question 93: D. 200,000

Question 94: B. Don Hutson died at age 84.

Question 95: Clark Hinkle Field and Ray Nitschke Field

Question 96: C. Favre's 7-year contract was the longest in franchise history.

Question 97: Holmgren Way

Question 98: B. 1950

Question 99: D. 55,000

Question 100: A. Minnesota Vikings

Question 101: The win earned the Packers a first round bye and gave them home field advantage for the divisional playoff.

Question 102: Denver Broncos

Question 103: C. 800 million

Question 104: B. 25,000 fans

Question 105: A. 61

Question 106: D. $24 million. 18,707 shareholders attended a meeting at Lambeau Field on July 8, 1998.

Question 107: Japan (Tokyo Dome)

Question 108: C. 25

Question 109: A. Minnesota Vikings

Question 110: B. 6

Question 111: D. 3 seconds

Question 112: Coach Mike Holmgren resigned to become vice president, general manager, and head coach of the Seattle Seahawks.

Question 113: Ray Rhodes

Question 114: D. 13

Question 115: 1993-1998

Question 116: B. 8th

Question 117: Camp Randall Stadium in Madison, Wisconsin

Keep a running tally of your correct answers!

Number correct: ___ / 48

Overall correct: ___ / 117

THE NEW MILLENNIUM

Question 118: In 2000, this head coach replaced Ray Rhodes to become the 13th head coach in franchise history. HINT: He was an offensive coordinator for Seattle and had been coaching for 21 years.

Question 119: Packers President Bob Harlan revealed plans to renovate Lambeau Field. How much were the proposed plans for?
  a) $175 million
  b) $225 million
  c) $265 million
  d) $295 million

Question 120: How did Governor Tommy Thompson help the Packers raise funds for the Lambeau Field renovation?

Question 121: Vice president and general manager Ron Wolf resigned. Whom did President Bob Harlan name to replace him as GM?

Question 122: Green Bay hosted the first Monday Night Football game after the 9/11 attacks. Who held the American flag for the national anthem?

Question 123: In 2002, the Packers beat the 49ers 25-15 in the NFC Wild Card matchup but were then pounded by the St. Louis Rams. What was the final score of the Rams' divisional playoff win?

Question 124: The next season the Packers clinched the NFC North divisional championship with four games left in the season when they defeated the Chicago Bears 30-20. However, they would go on to lose their first ever home playoff game. Who beat the Packers at home on January 4, 2003?

Question 125: On August 27, 2003, 14-foot statues of two Packers legends were unveiled. Name these legends.

Question 126: On September 7, 2003, with the help of two middle school students, commissioner Paul Tagliabue, and other special guests, the Packers rededicated Lambeau Field at halftime of their season opener against the Minnesota Vikings. True or False: The Packers won their season opener in their newly renovated stadium.

Question 127: Packers' running backs coach Sylvester Croom made Southeastern Conference history when he left the Packers organization to become head coach at Mississippi State University. Why was his move so historic?

Question 128: For the Packers "Rebirth of a Legend" event, legendary players returned to Lambeau Field to reenact what famous play?

Question 129: In 2003, Packers running back Ahman Green set a franchise record for most yards rushed in a single season. Whose record did he break?

Question 130: Who broke Don Hutson's Packers career scoring record?

Question 131: On December 22, 2003, Brett Favre gave the performance of his career when he threw for 399 yards and four touchdowns for a Monday Night win over Oakland. What else made this win and performance so special for Brett Favre?

Question 132: Green Bay clinched a playoff berth on the final game of the 2003 season when they beat Denver while Arizona somehow managed to beat Minnesota. How many wins did the Packers have in their last 9 games to accomplish this remarkable feat?
   a) 6
   b) 7
   c) 8
   d) 9

Question 133: Whose interception return helped the Packers beat the Seahawks in the NFC Wild Card playoff on January 4, 2004?

Question 134: One week later, the Packers came up just a few inches away from the NFC Championship when they lost 20-17 in overtime. Who beat them?

Question 135: John "Red" Cochran served the Packers organization for 42 years doing what before he passed away on September 5, 2004?

Question 136: On December 5, 2004, the Packers clinched their third straight NFC North championship when they beat the Minnesota Vikings 34-31 in Minnesota. Who scored the game winner in the closing seconds?

Question 137: Reggie White passed away in North Carolina on December 26, 2004. How did the Packers players pay homage to this legend who helped bring a Super Bowl championship back to Titletown?

Question 138: The Packers beat this team twice during the regular season but lost to them in the first round of the playoffs at Lambeau Field on January 9, 2005. Name this spoiler team.

Question 139: Whom did President Harlan name as the Packers new Executive Vice President, General Manager, and Director of Football Operations with complete authority over football decisions?

Question 140: The Packers organization held their first annual Green Bay Packers Fan Fest on March 11-13, 2005. What headline kicked off the weekend?

Question 141: In 2005, the Packers and American Family Insurance combined efforts to sell pink Packers hats to promote breast cancer awareness. Their goal was to raise $100,000 to help research and support those who are afflicted. How much did their initial efforts raise?
  a) $100,000
  b) $200,000
  c) $500,000
  d) $1,000,000

Question 142: On September 18, 2005, the Packers retired Reggie White's number 92. White's number was only the fifth number retired in franchise history. Name the other four legends whose numbers had been retired?

Question 143: On January 2, 2006, Ted Thompson fired coach Sherman only one day after the Packers suffered a 23-17 loss to Seattle. The Packers ended the season with a losing record. When was the last season the Packers finished below .500?

a) 1990

b) 1991

c) 1992

d) 1993

Question 144: How many days after firing Sherman did it take Thompson to name Mike McCarthy the Packers' 14th head coach in franchise history?

a) 3

b) 5

c) 7

d) 9

Question 145: What was the "Frozen Tundra Classic" that was played at Lambeau Field on February 11, 2006?

Question 146: Describe the "DD GrassMaster" surface that was put into Lambeau Field.

Question 147: Where did the Packers conduct their summer training camp practice on July 31, 2007? HINT: This was the first time they practiced there since August 5, 1961.

Question 148: On September 30, 2007, Brett Favre broke Dan Marino's NFL record for career touchdown passes. How many touchdown passes did Marino throw?

a) 403

b) 411

c) 420

d) 434

Question 149: Who did the Packers beat on December 9, 2007, to clinch their first NFC North title since 2004?

a) Minnesota Vikings

b) Chicago Bears

c) Detroit Lions

d) Oakland Raiders

Question 150: The Packers overcame a 14 point deficit to beat this team 42-20 in a snowy NFC divisional playoff on January 12, 2008.

Question 151: On January 20, 2007, the Packers lost a tough battle against the eventual Super Bowl champion New York Giants 23-20. What was the coldest the wind chill reached during this championship game?

a) 0
b) -1
c) -13
d) -23

Question 152: In 2008, the Packer Foundation awarded how much money in charity?

a) $1 million
b) $3 million
c) $5 million
d) $8 million

Question 153: On March 6, 2008, Brett Favre announced his retirement. How many games was he the starting quarterback for the Packers?

Question 154: A few months later Brett Favre un-retired. Who had to reinstate him before he could be traded to the New York Giants?

Question 155: On September 8, 2008, Aaron Rodgers became the first Packers quarterback to start other than Brett Favre since what year?

a) 1991
b) 1992
c) 1993
d) 1994

Question 156: How many assistant coaches did Mike McCarthy let go after the Packers dismissal 6-10 record in 2008?

a) 3
b) 4
c) 5
d) 6

Question 157: Whom did McCarthy hire to become his new defensive coordinator?

Question 158: Name the two first round draft choices the Packers picked in the 2009 NFL draft.

Question 159: What field did the Packers renovate in August of 2009 and name as their primary training-camp facility?

Question 160: What feat was a franchise first for the 2009 Packers defensive squad?

Question 161: The 2009 offense of the Packers also set a franchise record when they did what?

Question 162: On January 10, 2010, Green Bay lost in overtime to Arizona in the NFC Wildcard playoff. This game was the highest scoring playoff game in NFL history. What was the final score?

Question 163: On December 8, 2010, five Packers were selected for the Pro Bowl. After the alternates process, how many Packers actually represented the NFC in the all-star game?

    a) 6
    b) 7
    c) 8
    d) 9

Question 164: In 2010, the Packers won their final two regular season games to finish the season 10-6 and clinch the final playoff spot in the NFC. How many combined points did the Packers lose their six games by?

    a) 20
    b) 26
    c) 31
    d) 34

Question 165: True or False: The Packers never trailed a team by more than seven points during the entire 2010 season.

Question 166: What offensive powerhouse did the Packers beat on the road for their NFC Wildcard playoff win?

Question 167: On the road again, the Packers routed the top-seeded Atlanta Falcons in the divisional playoff. How many points did the Packers beat the

Falcons by?
   a) 18
   b) 21
   c) 24
   d) 27

Question 168: The Packers faced their rival Chicago Bears in the NFC Championship game on January 23, 2011. As of that game, how many times did these rivals face each other in the playoffs in their franchise histories?
   a) 2
   b) 5
   c) 7
   d) 10

Question 169: The Packers beat the Bears 21-14 and advanced to Super Bowl XLV. Where would they be playing for the Super Bowl title?

Question 170: Name the Packer who returned an interception late in the first quarter of Super Bowl XLV against the Pittsburgh Steelers.

Question 171: How many Steelers turnovers did the Packers defense force in Super Bowl XLV?

Question 172: The Packers defense held the Steelers on their final possession securing the Packers 31-25 win and their fourth Super Bowl title! How many world championships did this give the Packers franchise?
   a) 11
   b) 12
   c) 13
   d) 14

Question 173: Who was named Super Bowl XLV MVP?

Question 174: How many fans welcomed the Super Bowl champion Packers back to Green Bay at the "Return to Titletown" celebration at Lambeau Field despite below zero wind chill temperatures?
   a) 42,000
   b) 48,000
   c) 56,000

d) 62,000

Question 175: What was unique about when the Packers received their Super Bowl rings at Lambeau Field on June 16, 2011?

Question 176: The Super Bowl champion Packers visited the White House to be recognized by President Barack Obama. The Packers presented President Obama with a Packers jersey, but they also gave him one other unique gift. What was the other gift?

Question 177: On August 25, 2011, the Packers announced plans to add 6,700 seats to Lambeau Field. What other renovation plans did they reveal?

Question 178: The Packers kicked off the 2011 season with an opening day win over the New Orleans Saints at Lambeau Field. What day of the week was this game played on?
   a) Thursday
   b) Saturday
   c) Sunday
   d) Monday

Question 179: The Packers started the 2011 season with the team's longest single season winning streak. How many games in a row did they win?
   a) 11
   b) 12
   c) 13
   d) 14

Question 180: True or False: If you add the Packers' six wins in a row to close out their 2010 Super Bowl champion season to their 2011 start of the season winning streak, they would hold the longest winning streak in NFL history.

Question 181: True or False: Aaron Rodgers and the Packers offense scored 560 points during the 2011 regular season, establishing a new NFL record.

Question 182: The Packers had a first round bye but were then upset by the New York Giants 37-20 in the divisional playoff game on January 15, 2012.

How many turnovers did the Packers have?

a) 2
b) 3
c) 4
d) 5

Question 183: True or False: After the 2011 season, Aaron Rodgers was named the NFL's Most Valuable Player and was selected to be the starting quarterback for the NFC in the Pro Bowl.

Question 184: The NFL's referees started the 2012 season on strike. Many would argue that the Monday night game between the Green Bay Packers and the Seattle Seahawks ended the strike as fans demanded that the regular referees return to protect the integrity of the game. What Packers safety intercepted a desperation pass that was ruled a game-winning completion for Seahawks' receiver Golden Tate?

Question 185: What Wisconsin State Senator tweeted NFL commissioner Roger Goodell's office phone number?

Question 186: What former University of Kentucky quarterback recorded the most yards receiving for the 2012 Packers?

Question 187: What former University of Kentucky punter threw a 27-yard touchdown pass for the 2012 Packers?

Question 188: True or False: The Packers swept the Bears during the 2012 regular season.

Question 189: What team did the Packers pummel 55-7 on December 23, 2012?

a) Detroit Lions
b) Arizona Cardinals
c) St. Louis Rams
d) Tennessee Titans

Question 190: Despite the 2012 Packers 2-3 start, they managed to win the NFC North division. What was their final regular season record?

a) 9-7

b) 10-6
c) 11-5
d) 12-4

ANSWER KEY

Question 118: Mike Sherman

Question 119: D. $295 million

Question 120: While at Lambeau Field, Governor Tommy Thompson signed the state's stadium renovation bill into law allowing a .5% sales tax increase to help fund $160 million in construction bonds.

Question 121: Mike Sherman

Question 122: Both teams and members of Wisconsin police and fire departments helped hold the flag.

Question 123: 45-17

Question 124: Atlanta Falcons

Question 125: Vince Lombardi and Curly Lambeau

Question 126: False. Vikings won 30-25.

Question 127: Sylvester Croom became the SEC's first black head coach.

Question 128: Bart Starr's "Ice Bowl" quarterback sneak.

Question 129: Jim Taylor

Question 130: Ryan Longwell

Question 131: Brett Favre's father passed away a little over 24 hours before the game.

Question 132: B. 7

Question 133: Al Harris

Question 134: Philadelphia Eagles

Question 135: Assistant coach and scout. "Red" was still scouting when he died at the age of 82.

Question 136: Ryan Longwell

Question 137: Packers players wore a "92" decal on their helmets.

Question 138: Minnesota Vikings

Question 139: Ted Thompson

Question 140: Brett Favre announced that he would return for his 15th season.

Question 141: D. $1 million

Question 142: Tony Canadeo 3, Don Hutson 14, Bart Starr 15, Ray Nitschke 66.

Question 143: B. 1991

Question 144: D. 9 days

Question 145: The "Frozen Tundra Classic" was a hockey match between the University of Wisconsin Badgers and Ohio State Buckeyes. The near sell-out crowd of 40,890 fans watched the Badgers beat the Buckeyes 4-2. The Badgers went on to become the National Champions that year.

Question 146: The DD GrassMaster system consists of natural grass with manmade fibers. This system was installed at Lambeau Field above a new drainage and heating system in 2007.

Question 147: City Stadium. Approximately, 3,500 fans attended the practice.

Question 148: C. 420

Question 149: D. Oakland Raiders

Question 150: Seattle Seahawks

Question 151: D. -23 degrees. This was the third coldest temperature ever recorded at a divisional championship game.

Question 152: C. $5 million

Question 153: Brett Favre started 253 regular season games for the Packers. If you count playoff games, he started 275 games!

Question 154: NFL Commissioner Roger Goodell

Question 155: B. 1992

Question 156: D. 6

Question 157: Dom Capers

Question 158: Boston College's B.J. Raji was the 9th overall draft pick and USC's Clay Matthews was the 26th overall selection. The last time the Packers selected two first round picks was 1993.

Question 159: Nitschke Field

Question 160: The Packers finished first in the NFL for best defense against the run. They set a team record for allowing the fewest rushing yards per game.

Question 161: The Packers offense broke the team record for most points scored in a single season. The previous record was held by the 1996 Super Bowl championship team.

Question 162: Arizona 51 Green Bay 45

Question 163: 8 Packers represented the NFC in the Pro Bowl, the most the franchise has had since 1967.

Question 164: A. 20

Question 165: True. The Packers never trailed by more than seven points during the entire 2010 season!

Question 166: The Packers beat the Philadelphia Eagles 21-16.

Question 167: D. 27 points

Question 168: A. 2

Question 169: Cowboys Stadium in Arlington, Texas

Question 170: Nick Collins

Question 171: 3

Question 172: C. The Packers' 13 world championships are the most held by any football franchise.

Question 173: Aaron Rodgers. He threw for 304 yards and three touchdowns.

Question 174: C. 56,000

Question 175: Because of the ongoing labor negotiations between the players and the owners, the Packers players had to be granted a one-night exemption so they could receive their Super Bowl XLV championship rings.

Question 176: The Packers presented President Obama with a share of the Packers stock.

Question 177: The Packers released plans to add high-definition video screens and to add new elevator shafts.

Question 178: A. Thursday

Question 179: C. 13

Question 180: False. The 19-game winning streak was the second longest.

Question 181: False. 560 points was the second most points scored.

Question 182: C. 4 turnovers

Question 183: True.

Question 184: M.D. Jennings. Former NFL coach and ESPN analyst John Gruden called the officiating blunder both "tragic" and "comical." Before Tate caught Jennings who caught the ball, he clearly shoved Packers cornerback Sam Shields.

Question 185: State Senator Jon Erpenbach

Question 186: Randall Cobb

Question 187: Tim Masthay

Question 188: True

Question 189: D. Tennessee Titans

Question 190: C. 11-5

Keep a running tally of your correct answers!

Number correct: ___ / 73

Overall correct: ___ / 190

"Winning is a habit. Watch your thoughts, they become your beliefs. Watch your beliefs, they become your words. Watch your words, they become your actions. Watch your actions, they become your habits. Watch your habits, they become your character."

— *Vince Lombardi*

2 NFL HALL OF FAME PACKERS

Thousands of football fans grow up dreaming of someday playing in the NFL. Catching passes with friends and dads, eluding imaginary tacklers and lunging into end zones marked by Frisbees and fence posts, football players of all ages create images of themselves running onto a pro football field in front of crazed face-painted, chest-baring fans. And when these dreamers discover the hallowed Hall of Fame in Canton, Ohio, images of their bronzed faces and enshrined uniforms become their ultimate goal. Of course, of the hundreds of thousands who dream the dream, only a few thousand play college football while only a few hundred each year receive a contract to play in the NFL. Of those players, each year only a few are elected into the Hall of Fame. This chapter features the greatest Packers of all-time who have been elected into the NFL Hall of Fame, ensuring that their performances and personas will be immortalized for generations of fans.

Question 191: Counting Green Bay's two legendary Hall of Fame coaches, how many Packers are enshrined in the NFL Hall of Fame in Canton, Ohio?

    a) 12
    b) 17
    c) 19
    d) 21

Question 192: Name this Packers Hall of Famer who returned a 60-yard touchdown interception in Super Bowl II. This interception touchdown return was the only one recorded in the first 10 Super Bowl games. HINT: Throughout his career, some of which was played with the Dallas Cowboys, he returned 48 interceptions for 1,046 yards including 7 touchdowns.

Question 193: This ninth round draft choice from Gonzaga University played for the Packers from 1941 to 1952 but missed some playing time while serving in the Army during WWII. Name this Hall of Famer who was known for doing everything on the field including intercepting passes, passing, running, and returning punts and kickoffs.

Question 194: The Packers acquired this Hall of Famer from the Cleveland Browns in 1960. This player was surprised by the trade and considered quitting, but coach Vince Lombardi encouraged him saying, "I consider speed, agility and size to be the three most important attributes in a successful lineman. Give me a man who has two of those dimensions and he'll do okay. But give him all three and he'll be great. We think you have all three." Name this legend whose other attributes of dedication, leadership and durability made him one of football's all-time greats.

Question 195: In his book *Run to Daylight*, Vince Lombardi stated that this Packers Hall of Famer was the finest player he ever coached! This guard and tackle earned the "iron-man" nickname for playing in a then league record 188 consecutive games from 1956 until 1971.

Question 196: This Hall of Fame quarterback teamed with Don Hutson to form the first great pass-catch combo. In 1935, he connected with Hutson 18 times for 420 yards and 7 touchdowns. He was the NFL's passing leader in 1932, 1934, and 1936 and quarterbacked four Packers title teams. He was a football and basketball star at Green Bay West High School. He also was known to sell programs at early Packers games so he could watch. After college he worked in the Packers clubhouse as a handyman before coach Curly Lambeau decided to give the inexperienced player a tryout. Who is this quarterback who was the first to use the forward pass with such skill?

Question 197: Who is the Packers Hall of Famer who is known for doing everything well but was most recognized for being a vicious tackler, adept passer and wicked defender? HINT: He is most famous for his head-to-head battles with Chicago Bears rival Bronko Nagurski. His motto, "Get to Bronk before he gets to me" worked exceptionally well the day the Bears' icon was helped off the field with a broken nose and fractured rib.

Question 198: Where was Hall of Famer Paul "The Golden Boy" Hornung born?

Question 199: In what year did Hornung win the Heisman Trophy as the quarterback for the University of Notre Dame?
  a) 1955
  b) 1956
  c) 1957
  d) 1958

Question 200: Hornung was known for having a "nose for the end zone." Counting his touchdowns and PAT's and field goals as placekicker, how many points did he score for the Packers in his nine seasons?
  a) 670
  b) 720
  c) 760
  d) 810

Question 201: Name this Packers tackle Hall of Famer who stood 6 feet 2 inches and weighed 253 pounds making him a "huge" lineman by twenties and thirties' standards. In addition to his size, he could run the 100 yard dash in nearly 11 seconds. Known for his exceptional blocking, this legend helped lead Curly Lambeau's Packers to three consecutive titles in 1929, 1930, and 1931.

Question 202: This Packers Hall of Famer was named the NFL's all-time end. He held 18 NFL records at the time of his retirement in 1945. Who is this football icon?

Question 203: This defensive tackle became the fifth Packers player inducted into the Hall of Fame. This quick, intelligent defender was known for applying intense pressure to opposing quarterbacks. Who is this Hall of Famer who played on Lombardi's two Super Bowl title teams?

Question 204: Earl Louis "Curly" Lambeau is best known for founding the pre-NFL Packers in 1919 and coaching for 33 years, but he also was an outstanding quarterback and halfback. How many years did Lambeau play for the Packers?

    a) 10
    b) 11
    c) 12
    d) 13

Question 205: How many titles did Lambeau bring to Green Bay?

    a) 4
    b) 5
    c) 6
    d) 7

Question 206: At what university did Lambeau play fullback in his freshman year before an illness caused him to leave school?

    a) University of Notre Dame
    b) University of Southern California
    c) University of Alabama
    d) University of Arkansas

Question 207: Lambeau was the first pass-minded coach in the NFL, and he and his teams were described as impatient and explosive. Some considered him a "sometimes-hotheaded disciplinarian," but he retired as one of the winningest coaches of all-time. Counting his wins while coaching with the Chicago Cardinals and Washington Redskins, how many career wins did Lambeau have?

    a) 213
    b) 225
    c) 229
    d) 237

Question 208: Hall of Famer John McNally needed a nickname to protect his college eligibility when he left college one year early to try his hand at pro football. How did he decide on the nickname "Blood"?

Question 209: This Packers Hall of Famer recorded 50 receptions in a season 9 times. He also became the first NFL player to score a touchdown in the 1970s, 1980s, and 1990s.

Question 210: What Packer is the only player ever to be inducted into both the Pro Football Hall of Fame and Major League Baseball's Hall of Fame in Cooperstown, New York?

Question 211: True or False: Don Hutson's record of 99 touchdown receptions stood for over four decades.

Question 212: True or False: Vince Lombardi never coached a losing season.

Question 213: Vince Lombardi was declared the NFL's Man of the Decade in the 1960s. How many NFL titles did he win throughout his career?
   a) 5
   b) 6
   c) 7
   d) 8

Question 214: Lombardi coached the Packers in ten postseason games. Of those ten, how many did the Packers lose?
   a) 1
   b) 2
   c) 3
   d) 4

Question 215: True or False: When James Lofton retired after 16 seasons, he had caught 764 receptions for an NFL-record 14,004 yards.

Question 216: Who is this 60-minute workhorse who had a reputation for blitzing and helped the Packers line secure Green Bay's 1929, 1930, and 1931 championships? HINT: Because he played every minute of every game and was never injured he earned the nickname "Iron Mike".

Question 217: Who is the Packers legend who was named the NFL's all-time top linebacker because of his quickness and ruthless defense against rushes?

Question 218: Name this Packers Hall of Fame center who once held the record for playing in 182 consecutive games. He was known for playing through injuries. He played for the Packers from 1953-1963.

Question 219: This Hall of Famer played with the Packers for only one season in 1974, but he finished his career with 25 blocked field goals or PAT's and four safeties. HINT: He also played for the Baltimore Colts and the Oakland/Los Angeles Raiders.

Question 220: Who is the legendary offensive threat who also intercepted 30 passes in his final six seasons?

Question 221: What round was Hall of Fame quarterback Bart Starr drafted in?
   a) 1st round
   b) 3rd round
   c) 9th round
   d) 17th round

Question 222: Coach Lombardi was drawn to Starr's mechanics, arm, ball-handling techniques, and decision-making skills. What year did he win the NFL's Most Valuable Player award?
   a) 1961
   b) 1962
   c) 1964
   d) 1966

Question 223: True or False: When Starr retired after 16 years, his lifetime completion percentage of 57.4 percent was the NFL's all-time record.

Question 224: Some would argue Starr was at his best in his postseason games. The Packers lost only one playoff game under Starr's leadership. Name the only team to beat him in the postseason.

Question 225: Who is this Hall of Fame speedster who was an Academic All-American student athlete at Stanford University where he also won the NCAA long jump title?

Question 226: What Packers Hall of Famer was the basketball team captain at St. John's College and also lettered in football, baseball, and track?

Question 227: What Packer great was named Most Valuable Player in the 1962 NFL title game?

Question 228: Who once caught four touchdown passes in one quarter and kicked five PAT's scoring an astounding 29 points in one quarter for the Packers?

Question 229: This Lombardi era fullback was the Packers' "bread and butter guy" for gaining much-needed short yardage for first downs and touchdowns. Some considered him a throwback to football's earlier eras because of his tenacious and gutsy zeal on the football field.

Question 230: This Hall of Famer was a 5 feet 10 inch, 190-pound quarterback from the University of Southern California who was never drafted. After seeking a tryout with the Packers, he made the Packers squad as a safety and went on to intercept a pass from Kansas City Chief's Len Dawson and return it for 50-yards at a crucial time in Super Bowl I. Who is this Packers Hall of Fame safety?

Question 231: This Hall of Fame safety played for the Packers from 1959-1961 and became the first African-American inducted into the Pro Football Hall of Fame.

Question 232: Don Hutson signed contracts with two professional football teams. NFL President Joe Carr ruled that the contract with the earliest postmark would be honored. The Packers' contract postmarked at 8:30 A.M. was postmarked 17 minutes earlier than the other team's contract. Name the NFL team that was just a few minutes away from securing one of the NFL's greatest players of all-time.

Question 233: What Packer great passed on a professional baseball contract with the St. Louis Browns?

Question 234: This Packers Hall of Famer played for Syracuse University in the 1953 Orange Bowl but lost to Alabama 61-5! As a 20-year old Packers draftee, he nearly quit when he reported to Grand Rapids, Minnesota for training camp. However, his family would not take him back home saying that they did not want a quitter and he should at least try.

Question 235: What Packers great won NFL Most Valuable Player honors for two consecutive years in 1941 and 1942?

Question 236: What Packer ran for over 1,000 yards for five straight seasons starting in 1960?

Question 237: True or False: Reggie White acquired more career sacks than games played.

Question 238: Reggie White became the Packers all-time leading sacker. How many sacks did he record in the green and gold uniform?
   a) 68.5
   b) 71
   c) 74.5
   d) 78

Question 239: What was Reggie White's nickname?

Question 240: White was named to the NFL's All-Decade Teams of the 1980s and 1990s, the 75th Anniversary Team, and was voted First-Team All-Pro 10 times in his 15 years of NFL football. He retired as the NFL's all-time leading sacker. How many sacks did he record for the Eagles, Packers, and his one year with the Carolina Panthers?
   a) 178
   b) 186
   c) 198
   d) 201.5

Question 241: Jim Taylor ran the ball for 85 yards and scored the Packers only touchdown in the 1962 title game against the New York Giants. At the end of the game, he could barely see and barely talk. What injuries did he sustain?

Question 242: A game ball from Super Bowl XXXI is on display in the Hall of Fame. What two Packers signatures are on this ball?

Question 243: Why is Brett Favre's Minnesota Vikings jersey from the

December 6, 2009, game against the Arizona Cardinals on display in the Hall of Fame?

Question 244: What Packer has the honor of having his 2009 uniform on display in the Hall of Fame?

Question 245: Tony Canadeo's helmet that he started wearing in 1941 is on display at the Hall of Fame. What number was written on the front of it?

Question 246: Why is Randall Cobb's jersey from the 2011 home opener against the New Orleans Saints in the Hall of Fame?

Question 247: Where did the Packers conduct their summer training camp practice on July 31, 2007? HINT: This was the first time they practiced there since August 5, 1961.

Question 248: Brett Favre's jerseys from when he broke the NFL all-time passing yard record (2007) and when he set the record for 117th consecutive start at quarterback (1999) are on display in the Hall of Fame? What is significant about his 1994 jersey that is also on display?

Question 249: The Hall of Fame displays some incredibly valuable relics such as Don Hutson's 1945 game-used jersey and a 1929 Green Bay Packers autographed football. However, it does have some rather interesting artifacts like Clarke Hinkle's stadium blanket and a box of sod from Lambeau Field. What remnant from the historic "Ice Bowl" made the Hall of Fame displays?

Question 250: Sterling Sharpe set the record for most receptions in a single season in 1993. What did he donate to the Hall of Fame to commemorate this accomplishment?

ANSWER KEY

Question 191: D. 21

Question 192: Herb Adderley. Adderley, a Michigan State star running back, became a cornerback midway through his rookie season because he was competing against future Hall of Famers Jim Taylor and Paul Hornung.

Question 193: Tony Canadeo. Canadeo averaged 75 all-purpose yards a game throughout his 116 game career.

Question 194: Willie Davis

Question 195: Forrest Gregg

Question 196: Arnie Herber

Question 197: Clarke Hinkle. When Hinkle retired in 1941, he was the NFL's all-time leading rusher.

Question 198: Louisville, Kentucky

Question 199: B. 1956

Question 200: C. 760 points. Hornung once scored five touchdowns in one game against the Baltimore Colts in 1965.

Question 201: Cal Hubbard

Question 202: Don Hutson

Question 203: Henry Jordan

Question 204: B. 11

Question 205: C. 6

Question 206: A. Notre Dame

Question 207: C. 229 wins

Question 208: John "Blood" McNally passed a movie theater that was featuring the film *Blood and Sand*. McNally declared, "That's it. You be Sand. I'll be Blood."

Question 209: James Lofton

Question 210: Cal Hubbard. Hubbard became a respected Major League Baseball umpire and was named the American League's umpire-in-chief in 1958.

Question 211: True

Question 212: True. When Lombardi became the Packers head coach in 1959, the Packers had just completed a very dismal 1-10-1 season. At the team's first meeting, Lombardi stated, "I have never been on a losing team, gentlemen, and I do not intend to start now!" The Packers then went 7-5 in 1959. Lombardi nearly duplicated this feat when he took over as head coach of the struggling Washington Redskins and coached them to a 7-5-2 record in his first season with the franchise.

Question 213: A. 5 titles

Question 214: A. 1

Question 215: True

Question 216: Mike Michalske

Question 217: Ray Nitschke

Question 218: Jim Ringo

Question 219: Ted Hendricks

Question 220: Don Hutson

Question 221: D. 17th round

Question 222: D. 1966

Question 223: True

Question 224: Philadelphia Eagles (1960)

Question 225: James Lofton

Question 226: John "Blood" McNally. Blood's wife once said, "Even when Johnny does the expected, he does it in an unexpected way."

Question 227: Ray Nitschke

Question 228: Don Hutson (1945)

Question 229: Jim Taylor. Lombardi described Taylor as the most determined runner he had ever seen. In addition to his intense running, Taylor is also remembered for his powerful blocks.

Question 230: Willie Wood. Wood intercepted 48 passes throughout his career and returned them for 699 yards.

Question 231: Emlen Tunnell

Question 232: Brooklyn Dodgers

Question 233: Ray Nitschke

Question 234: Jim Ringo

Question 235: Don Hutson

Question 236: Jim Taylor. Taylor ran for a career best 1,474 yards in 1962 and was named the NFL's Player of the Year.

Question 237: False. Although White accomplished this feat during his years with the Philadelphia Eagles with 124 sacks in 121 games, he was not able to maintain that pace throughout the rest of his career.

Question 238: A. 68.5. White also recorded 3 sacks in Super Bowl XXXI.

Question 239: "Minister of Defense." White became an ordained minister at the age of 17.

Question 240: C. 198

Question 241: Taylor's cut elbow required 7 stitches at halftime, and he also endured a severely cut tongue.

Question 242: The game ball was signed my Super Bowl MVP Desmond Howard and coach Mike Holmgren.

Question 243: This was Favre's 283rd consecutive NFL game played breaking the record previously held by the Vikings' Jim Marshall.

Question 244: Charles Woodson. Woodson's 2009 season resulted in an NFL record tying 9 interceptions, and he was voted the NFL's Defensive Player of the Year. This was only the second time a Packer earned this honor; Reggie White also accomplished this feat in 1998.

Question 245: 3

Question 246: The DD GrassMaster system consists of natural grass with manmade fibers. This system was installed at Lambeau Field above a new drainage and heating system in 2007.

Question 247: City Stadium. Approximately 3,500 fans attended the practice.

Question 248: C. 420

Question 249: D. Oakland Raiders

Question 250: Sharpe donated the football and his gloves.

Keep a running tally of your correct answers!

Number correct: ___ / 60

Overall correct: ___ / 250

"There's only one way to succeed in anything, and that is to give it everything. I do, and I demand that my players do."

— *Vince Lombardi*

3 GREEN BAY PACKERS HALL OF FAME LEGENDS

During the summer of 1967, William Brault opened the Green Bay Packers Hall of Fame in Green Bay, Wisconsin, because he realized Green Bay residents and tourists wanted to learn more about and recognize the Packers historic franchise. Only 21 Packers are in the NFL Hall of Fame in Canton, Ohio; however, since 1970, 148 Packers greats have been inducted into the Packers Hall of Fame. It first opened in the concourse of the Brown County Veterans Memorial Arena. All of the questions in this section feature players, coaches, announcers, and other important Packers figures who have been inducted into the Green Bay Packers Hall of Fame.

Question 251: What 6 feet 3 inch 250 pound Packer kicked three field goals to the help Green Bay win the 1962 title game 16-7 in New York?

Question 252: The Green Bay Packers Hall of Fame was dedicated in its new facility with the help of what political figure?

Question 253: What Packers running back from Texas Tech signed for $600,000 in 1967, the highest in the NFL at that time? HINT: His nickname was the "Golden Palomino."

Question 254: What Packers running back ran for 1,067 yards in a season in which he also caught 61 passes for 648 yards?

a) Jim Taylor
b) Ahman Green
c) Sterling Sharpe
d) Don Hutson

Question 255: What Packers fan-favorite and powerful nose tackle was known as the "Gravedigger"?

Question 256: At 6 feet 1 inch, this 200 pound defender made a name for himself as a smart, innovative cornerback. He also averaged 25 yards on kickoff returns throughout his career. HINT: He intercepted a Daryle Lamonica pass and returned it for 60 yards in Super Bowl II.

Question 257: What running back helped the Packers secure titles in 1931, 1936 and 1939?

Question 258: Who is the veteran quarterback who came to Green Bay to become an important backup during the Lombardi era and later served the Packers organization as an assistant coach?

Question 259: Who is the steady Packers center of nine years who went to the 1996 Pro Bowl? His nickname was "Bag of Donuts."

Question 260: What announcer teamed up with Tony Canadeo in 1956 to broadcast the Packers televised games?

Question 261: Who is the Packers center who started in the 1963 Rose Bowl for the University of Wisconsin Badgers? HINT: He and Jerry Kramer helped open the hole for Bart Starr's quarterback sneak touchdown in the 1967 championship.

Question 262: This tenacious and tough defensive back survived extreme poverty as a child growing up in Jacksonville, Florida. Growing up, he also overcame serious foot and leg injuries that at one point confined him to a wheelchair. Who is this player who was named to the NFL's All-Decade 1990s Team?

Question 263: Who is the 5 feet 8 inch lineman who used a lot of heart and hard hitting to make up for his lack of size? HINT: He played on the 1939 and 1944 title teams.

Question 264: What running back/returner set an NFL record in 1956 for 927 yards on kickoff returns, including his 106 yard return against the Chicago Bears?

Question 265: Name the tight end whose 25 postseason catches for 259 yards and four touchdowns are the best in franchise history.

Question 266: What Packer great also wrote books such as *Instant Replay*, *Distant Replay*, and *Lombardi: Winning is the Only Thing*?

Question 267: What 6 foot 5 inch, 235 pound Lombardi first round draft pick helped redefine the tall, faster linebacker era? HINT: He also played basketball on the 1966 NCAA National Champions University of Texas El Paso.

Question 268: Name this gritty safety who set a Packers record with 37 punt returns for 307 yards and became a teacher after his NFL career ended with the Packers.

Question 269: Why was Jerry Kramer's nickname "Zipper"?

Question 270: Curly Lambeau went to Green Bay East High School. What college did he attend and under whom did he play football during his freshman year?

Question 271: Name the Packers running back who ran for four touchdowns against the Arizona Cardinals on January 2, 2000.

Question 272: What young quarterback replaced Randy Wright and helped the Packers finish 10-6 in 1989, their best record since 1972?

Question 273: Johnny "Blood" McNally was well known for bizarre antics like hanging from a ship's flagpole on a Packers trip to Hawaii, climbing on top of a moving train, and jumping across a ledge six stories high to enter a Los Angeles hotel. He is said to have been part of the inspiration behind a George Clooney movie. Name this football film.

Question 274: What other nickname did Johnny "Blood" McNally earn because he played for so many different teams?

Question 275: Name the two brother centers/linebackers who played for the Packers in the late 1930s.

Question 276: Fred "Fuzzy" Thurston played on five Packers championship teams from 1959 through 1967. He is a Wisconsin native. Name his hometown.
   a) Altoona
   b) Appleton
   c) Ripon
   d) Sheboygan

Question 277: In 1992, the Packers defense was ranked 23rd in the NFL. The next year after adding Reggie White to the team, what did their ranking improve to?
   a) 8th
   b) 6th
   c) 4th
   d) 3rd

Question 278: How many times was Don Hutson named First-Team All-Pro?

Question 279: Name this Packers center who played in 162 consecutive games, the most in Packers history, earning him the nickname "The Rock."

Question 280: Name this legend who is among Packers career leaders in tackles (926) and unassisted tackles (687). He was voted Packers rookie of the Year by Wisconsin Sports media in 1981 after replacing an injured Johnnie Gray.

Question 251: Jerry Kramer

Question 252: President Gerald R. Ford

Question 253: Donny Anderson

Question 254: Edgar Bennett

Question 255: Gilbert Brown

Question 256: Herb Adderley

Question 257: Hank Bruden

Question 258: Zeke Bratkowski

Question 259: Frank Winters

Question 260: Ray Scott

Question 261: Ken Bowman

Question 262: LeRoy Butler

Question 263: Pete Tinsley

Question 264: Al Carmichael

Question 265: Mark Chmura

Question 266: Jerry Kramer

Question 267: Fred Carr

Question 268: Johnnie Gray

Question 269: Jerry Kramer's nickname "Zipper" was given to him by his teammates because of all of his injuries and scars.

Question 270: Notre Dame, Knute Rockne (1918)

Question 271: Dorsey Levens

Question 272: Don "The Majik Man" Majkowski. Majkowski threw for 4,318 yards and 27 touchdowns in 1989 and was named to the Pro Bowl. He was injured during the third game of the 1992 season and was replaced by Brett Favre. Favre helped the Packers beat the Bengals 24-23 that day.

Question 273: *Leatherheads*

Question 274: "The Vagabond Back"

Question 275: Earl "Bud" Svendsen and George Svendsen. Brother "Bud" intercepted a pass from Lem Barnum in the 1939 championship game played at Milwaukee State Fair Grounds.

Question 276: A. Altoona

Question 277: D. 3rd

Question 278: 8

Question 279: Larry McCarren

Question 280: Mark Murphy

Keep a running tally of your correct answers!

Number correct: ___ / 30

Overall correct: ___ / 280

"If you aren't fired with enthusiasm, you'll be fired with enthusiasm."
— *Vince Lombardi*

4 PACKERS RECORDS

Few franchises have such a rich tradition as the Green Bay Packers. If a Packers player holds a franchise record, he can be assured that his achievement will immortalize him amongst some of the game's all-time greats. From Hutson to Rodgers, most of the Packers records are here to challenge you and help you track what records are about to be broken by up-and-comers like Randall Cobb, Jordy Nelson and Clay Matthews.

Some say records are made to be broken, yet a frequent topic among fans is what records will never be broken. A statue of the St. Louis Cardinals legendary slugger Stan "The Man" Musial reads, "He holds many records." Regardless of whether a record is embossed under a statue or written on a dry erase board high up on a high school gymnasium's wall, a record is a record and worth noting. This chapter features some Packers records that are fascinating facts certain to raise your Green Bay Packers IQ.

Question 281: True or False: Brett Favre and Bart Starr share the record for most seasons played with the Green Bay Packers.

Question 282: Who holds the Packers record for most career touchdowns?
  a) Jim Taylor
  b) Ahman Green
  c) Sterling Sharpe
  d) Don Hutson

Question 283: Who holds the Packers record for most touchdowns in a season?

a) Jim Taylor

b) Ahman Green

c) Sterling Sharpe

d) Don Hutson

Question 284: What Packers rookie scored 13 touchdowns in his rookie season?

a) Max McGee

b) Gerry Ellis

c) Billy Howton

d) Samkon Gado

Question 285: Who has the most career punts for the Packers?

a) Don Bracken

b) David Beverley

c) Donny Anderson

d) Josh Bidwell

Question 286: How many of Mason Crosby's first 258 PAT's did he miss?

a) 6

b) 4

c) 3

d) 2

Question 287: Who holds the Packers record for most career yards rushing with 8,322?

a) Jim Taylor

b) Ahman Green

c) John Brockington

d) Don Hutson

Question 288: Ahman Green holds the longest run from scrimmage in Packers history. How long was this record-setting run?

a) 99 yards

b) 98 yards

c) 97 yards

d) 96 yards

Question 289: What Packers rookie rushed for 1,105 yards?
   a) Gerry Ellis
   b) Ahman Green
   c) John Brockington
   d) Samkon Gado

Question 290: How many times has a Packer player rushed for over 200 yards in a game?

Question 291: What Packer was the league's leading rusher in 1928 and 1930?

Question 292: True or False: Aaron Rodgers' 2011 passer rating of 122.5 is the highest ever recorded in NFL history.

Question 293: True or False: Brett Favre's single passer rating of 154.9 against the Oakland Raiders on December 22, 2003, is the highest ever rating for a Packers quarterback in franchise history.

Question 294: True or False: Don Majkowski's 59 pass attempts against the Detroit Lions on November 2, 1989, are the most ever attempted by a Packers quarterback in a single game.

Question 295: Brett Favre threw for an amazing 61,655 yards for the Packers! How many yards did he throw throughout his entire career?
   a) 66,784
   b) 68,236
   c) 70,348
   d) 71,838

Question 296: How many of Brett Favre's 16 seasons did he throw for over 3,000 yards?
   a) 16
   b) 15
   c) 14
   d) 13

Question 297: True or False: Brett Favre never threw more than Lynn Dickey's 4,458 yards in a season.

Question 298: Quarterback Cecil Isbell connected with Don Hutson for the shortest Packers completion ever recorded. How many inches was it?
a) 4
b) 6
c) 8
d) 9

Question 299: Brett Favre holds the Packers record for most career touchdown passes with 442. He also holds the NFL all-time record. How many touchdown passes did he throw throughout his NFL career?
a) 502
b) 508
c) 515
d) 518

Question 300: Aaron Rodgers broke Brett Favre's record for most touchdowns in a season. How many touchdowns did he throw for in 2011?
a) 41
b) 43
c) 45
d) 47

Question 301: Neither Brett Favre nor Aaron Rodgers has ever thrown for 6 touchdowns in a game. Name the only quarterback in Packers franchise history to accomplish this incredible feat.

Question 302: Bart Starr holds the Packers record for most consecutive pass attempts without an interception. How many attempts did he go without an interception?
a) 212
b) 238
c) 267
d) 294

Question 303: In 1966, Bart Starr threw only 3 interceptions in 251 attempts. How many did Aaron Rodgers throw in 2011 on 502 attempts?

    a) 6

    b) 7

    c) 8

    d) 9

Question 304: Who is the unfortunate Packers quarterback who threw for 6 interceptions in a game with only 15 attempts?

    a) Randy Wright

    b) Jack Jacobs

    c) Tom O'Malley

    d) Tobin Rote

Question 305: After the 2011 season, Aaron Rodgers had thrown only 38 interceptions in 2,223 career attempts. True or False: His 1.80% was the lowest career percentage in NFL history.

Question 306: What Packers receiver holds the franchise record of 735 receptions?

    a) Sterling Sharpe

    b) Don Hutson

    c) Donald Driver

    d) James Lofton

Question 307: Sterling Sharpe caught 112 passes in 1993 and 108 passes in 1992. Name the only other Packers receiver to catch over 100 passes in a season.

Question 308: Who kicked a 58 yard field goal, the longest in Packers franchise history?

    a) Ryan Longwell

    b) Mason Crosby

    c) Chris Jacke

    d) Jan Stenerud

Question 309: How many 50+ yard field goals did Chris Jacke kick for the Packers?

    a) 15

b) 16
c) 17
d) 19

Question 310: Willie Davis recorded two safeties for the Packers. Name the only other Packers player to record two safeties for the Packers. Amazingly, this player completed the two safeties in the same season.

Question 311: Put the following four receivers in order of most career yards received for the Packers: Donald Driver, Donald Hutson, James Lofton and Sterling Sharpe.

Question 312: Put the following four receivers in order of most yards received in a season for the Packers: Robert Brooks, Antonio Freeman, Sterling Sharpe and Javon Walker.

Question 313: What Packers receiver once caught seven passes for 257 yards in a single game?

Question 314: What Packers receiver caught the most 100 or more yards games?
    a) James Lofton
    b) Sterling Sharpe
    c) Don Hutson
    d) Donald Driver

Question 315: What Packers receiver caught 18 touchdown passes in one season?
    a) James Lofton
    b) Sterling Sharpe
    c) Don Hutson
    d) Donald Driver

Question 316: What two Packers caught 4 touchdown passes in one game?
    a) James Lofton
    b) Sterling Sharpe
    c) Don Hutson
    d) Donald Driver

Question 317: What Packer broke Ahman Green's record for all-purpose yards in a season?

Question 318: What two years did Charles Woodson lead the league in interceptions?

Question 319: What college did Heisman trophy winner Charles Woodson attend?

Question 320: What Packer has the most career interceptions?
  a) Leroy Butler
  b) Bobby Dillon
  c) Willie Wood
  d) Charles Woodson

Question 321: What Packers defender intercepted an NFL record four passes in one game?
  a) Leroy Butler
  b) Bobby Dillon
  c) Willie Wood
  d) Charles Woodson

Question 322: What Packer has the most interceptions returned for a touchdown?
  a) Leroy Butler
  b) Irv Comp
  c) Nick Collins
  d) Charles Woodson

Question 323: Who is the only Packer who can boast about intercepting a pass in five consecutive games?
  a) Leroy Butler
  b) Irv Comp
  c) Nick Collins
  d) Charles Woodson

Question 324: What Packers punter has the highest average punt for a season?
  a) Craig Hentrich

b) Jerry Norton

c) Jon Ryan

d) Tim Masthay

Question 325: Who recorded the longest punt in Packers franchise history?

a) Don Chandler

b) Jack Jacobs

c) Boyd Dowler

d) Tim Masthay

Question 326: Who is the only Packers player to lead the league in punt returns?

Question 327: Randall Cobb's kickoff return against the New Orleans Saints on September 8, 2011, is considered to be longest kickoff return in NFL history. How long was it?

Question 328: What Packer returned an NFL record four kickoffs for a touchdown in one season?

a) Dave Hampton

b) Roell Preston

c) Travis Williams

d) Darrell Thompson

Question 329: What Packers defender is the only Packer to lead the team in tackles for five seasons?

a) A.J. Hawk

b) Nick Barnett

c) Brian Noble

d) Bernardo Harris

Question 330: Who has the most career tackles for the Packers?

a) John Anderson

b) Nick Barnett

c) Johnnie Gray

d) Leroy Butler

Question 331: What Packer has the most career fumble recoveries?

a) Johnnie Gray

b) Ray Nitschke
c) Willie Davis
d) Mike Douglass

Question 332: Who is the only Packer to return 3 fumbles for a touchdown?
a) Keith McKenzie
b) Mike Douglass
c) LeRoy Butler
d) Darren Sharper

Question 333: Who is the all-time leading sack man for the Packers?
a) Reggie White
b) Tim Harris
c) Kabeer Gbaja-Biamila
d) Aaron Kampman

Question 334: What Packer recorded a franchise record 19.5 sacks in one season?
a) Reggie White
b) Tim Harris
c) Kabeer Gbaja-Biamila
d) Aaron Kampman

Question 335: What Packers rookie sacked 10 quarterbacks during his rookie season?

Question 336: What Packer once sacked the Buffalo Bills five times in one game? Note: Ezra Johnson (9/378) and Dave Pureifory (12/14/75) each recorded 5 sacks in a game before the sack became an official statistic.
a) Reggie White
b) Vonnie Holliday
c) Bryce Paup
d) Alphonso Carreker

Question 337: What Packer boasts an NFL record 7 blocked kicks in a season?
a) Ken Ellis

b) Ted Hendricks

c) Gary Lewis

d) Charles "Buckets" Goldenberg

Question 338: On October 7, 1945, the Packers set an NFL record that still stands today for most points scored in a quarter. How many points did they score during the second quarter of a 57-21 victory against Detroit on that day?

a) 34

b) 37

c) 40

d) 41

Question 339: The Packers also hold an NFL record for most points scored in one half. How many points did they score during the first half of a 55-14 victory against Tampa Bay on October 2, 1983?

a) 45

b) 47

c) 49

d) 51

Question 340: Who are the highest scoring touchdown combinations in franchise history?

a) Brett Favre-Antonio Freeman

b) Brett Favre-Donald Driver

c) Brett Favre-Sterling Sharpe

d) Lynn Dickey-Paul Coffman

Question 281: True. Both Brett Favre and Bart Starr played in 16 seasons for the Packers. However, Favre played in 255 games while Starr played in 196.

Question 282: D. Don Hutson

Question 283: B. Ahman Green

Question 284: C. Billy Howton

Question 285: Clay Matthews

Question 286: D. 2 Crosby had a 99.22% at the start of the 2012 season.

Question 287: B. Ahman Green

Question 288: B. 98 yards

Question 289: C. John Brockington

Question 290: Only one time has a Packers player rushed for over 200 yards. Ahman Green ran for 218 yards against the Denver Broncos on December 28, 2003.

Question 291: Verne Lewellen

Question 292: True

Question 293: False. Rodgers posted a 155.4 passer rating on October 25, 2009.

Question 294: False. Favre attempted 61 passes on October 14, 1996.

Question 295: D. Brett Favre threw for 71,838 career yards, an NFL record that will likely stand for all-time.

Question 296: A. 16. Favre threw for over 3,000 yards in 18 NFL seasons.

Question 297: True. The most Favre ever threw in a season was 4,413. However, Aaron Rodgers broke the franchise record in 2011 with 4,643 yards.

Question 298: A. 4 inches

Question 299: B. 508

Question 300: C. 45

Question 301: Matt Flynn threw for 6 touchdowns against the Detroit Lions on January 1, 2012.

Question 302: D. 294

Question 303: A. 6. Coincidentally, that is the exact same percentage!

Question 304: C. Tom O'Malley (September 17, 1950)

Question 305: True

Question 306: C. Donald Driver

Question 307: Robert Brooks caught 102 passes in 1995.

Question 308: B. Mason Crosby

Question 309: C. 17

Question 310: Tim Harris (1988) Two safeties in one season is an NFL record.

Question 311: Donald Driver (10,060), James Lofton (9,656), Sterling Sharpe (8,134) and Don Hutson (7,991)

Question 312: Robert Brooks (1497), Sterling Sharpe (1,461), Antonio Freeman (1,424) and Javon Walker (1,382)

Question 313: Billy Howton (10/21/56)

Question 314: A. James Lofton (32)

Question 315: B. Sterling Sharpe (1994)

Question 316: B. Sterling Sharpe and C. Don Hutson

Question 317: Randall Cobb (2012)

Question 318: 2009, 2011

Question 319: Charles Woodson became the third Heisman Trophy Award winner from the University of Michigan.

Question 320: B. Bobby Dillon 1952-59 (52)

Question 321: B. Bobby Dillon 11/26/53

Question 322: D. Charles Woodson

Question 323: B. Irv Comp (1943)

Question 324: D. Tim Masthay 45.6 average (2011)

Question 325: A. Don Chandler's 90-yard punt against San Francisco on October 10, 1965, is a Packers franchise record.

Question 326: Desmond Howard's 58 returns for 875 yards in 1996 is an NFL record.

Question 327: 108 yards

Question 328: C. Travis Williams accomplished this feat in his rookie season!

Question 329: B. Nick Barnett

Question 330: A. John Anderson 1,020 (1978-1989)

Question 331: C. Willie Davis

Question 332: B. Mike Douglass

Question 333: C. Kabeer Gbaja-Biamila

Question 334: B. Tim Harris (1989)

Question 335: Clay Matthews (2009)

Question 336: B. Vonnie Holliday

Question 337: B. Ted Hendricks

Question 338: D. 41

Question 339: C. 49

Question 340: A. Brett Favre – Antonio Freeman

Keep a running tally of your correct answers!

Number correct: ___ / 60

Overall correct: ___ / 340

"After all the cheers have died down and the stadium is empty, after the headlines have been written, and after you are back in the quiet of your room and the championship ring has been placed on the dresser and after all the pomp and fanfare have faded, the enduring thing that is left is the dedication to doing with our lives the very best we can to make the world a better place in which to live."

— *Vince Lombardi*

5 EXTRA POINTS

Unfortunately, 350 questions are not enough to fully capture the essence of the Green Bay Packers historic franchise and their frenzied fans. Questions like, "What fan decided taking his shirt off in the zero degree frozen tundra weather was the best way to support the team and why did hundreds of fans for all these years join him in this tradition?" are not in here. Consider these last questions a fourth and inches play that hopefully will allow you to Bart Starr-like quarterback sneak your way into the end zone and catapult you into ultimate fan status.

Question 341: Coach Lombardi is famous for saying, "If you are on time you are late. The clock at Lambeau Field is set on "Lombardi Time." How many minutes early is the clock set?
   a) 5 minutes
   b) 10 minutes
   c) 15 minutes
   d) 20 minutes

Question 342: Who is the only Packers player to make the Pro Bowl each of his first four seasons?

Question 343: What was Aaron Rodgers' quarterback rating when he was injured in November 2013?
   a) 93

b) 101

c) 108

d) 122

Question 344: Through the 2011 season, the Packers completed 21 of 36 two-point conversion attempts. True or False: During the same period, the Packers have held their opponents to under 50% of their two-point conversion attempts.

Question 345: True or False: Aaron Rodgers recorded the league's best quarterback rating in 2012 for the second season in a row.

Question 346: James Jones led the league with the most touchdown passes caught during the 2012 season. How many touchdown passes did he catch?

a) 12

b) 13

c) 14

d) 16

Question 347: The Packers beat the Minnesota Vikings 24-10 in the 2013 Wild Card Playoff. Aaron Rodgers set an NFL postseason record for completing passes to the most receivers. How many different Packers caught a pass from Rodgers on January 5, 2013?

a) 8

b) 9

c) 10

d) 11

Question 348: Aaron Rodgers threw an interception to Tarell Brown of the San Francisco 49ers in the first half of the 2013 Divisional Playoff. This was Rodgers' first interception in over 5 games. How many passes did he go without an interception?

a) 164

b) 172

c) 179

d) 183

Question 349: Aaron Rodgers threw a 3-yard touchdown pass to Greg

Jennings with 57 seconds left in the Packers 45-31 2013 Divisional Playoff loss to the San Francisco 49ers. What was significant about this Jennings touchdown?

Question 350: If you travel to Green Bay and take the Heritage Trail Foundation's city walk self-guided tour, how many Green Bay Packers commemorative plaques could you expect to see informing you about Packers history?

ANSWER KEY

Question 341: D. 20 minutes

Question 342: Clay Matthews

Question 343: C. 108

Question 344: False. Packers' opponents have completed exactly 50% of their two-point conversion attempts through the 2011 season. (33 of 66)

Question 345: True

Question 346: C. 14

Question 347: C. 10

Question 348: D. 183

Question 349: The touchdown reception to Jennings moved him into first place on the Packers all-time leading postseason receptions list. That gave him 50, passing Donald Driver with 49.

Question 350: There are 22 bronze plaques that make up the self-guided Packers Heritage Trail.

Keep a running tally of your correct answers!

Number correct: ___ / 10

Overall correct: ___ / 350

GREEN BAY PACKERS IQ

300-350
Super Bowl Champ and Hall of Famer

250-299
Conference Champ and League MVP

200-249
Pro Bowl

150-199
Practice Squad

149 & below
A Bears Fan

JOEL KATTE

ABOUT THE AUTHOR

Joel Katte is an elementary school principal for Fayette County Public Schools in Lexington, Kentucky.

Joel loves taking road trips with his family. He and his family enjoy hiking, biking, swimming, and playing tennis. During summers, Joel also plays baseball for the Lexington Bombers in the Bluegrass Baseball League.

Joel's first book, *Milwaukee Brewers IQ: The Ultimate Test of True Fandom*, was a #1 best-selling baseball book on Amazon. In the near future he hopes to publish his memoir *The County Stadium Kid* along with more IQ Series titles. For updates follow Joel on Twitter @joelkatte or visit:

www.KentuckyDerbyIQ.blogspot.com
www.CountyStadiumKid.blogspot.com
JoelKatte@gmail.com

Visit us on the web to learn more about Black Mesa and our authors:

www.blackmesabooks.com

Or contact us via email:

admin@blackmesabooks.com

REFERENCES

WEBSITES
ESPN.go.com
NFL.com
Packers.com
Packershalloffame.com
Packersheritagetrail.com
Profootballhof.com
Pro-football-reference.com
Vincelombardi.com

JOEL KATTE

Milwaukee Brewers IQ:
The Ultimate Test of True Fandom

JOEL KATTE

Available from Black Mesa Publishing.

"I've never been much on stats. Usually those things don't cross my mind as much as helping the team win. I've never set goals for myself. The only goal I've ever really thought about is to win the World Series."

— *Robin Yount*

1 SPRING TRAINING

This is Spring Training mind you. We're only stretching here. Just trying to get limber after a long winter of chips, couches, remote controls, beverages of choice and the NFL ... I mean there's no sense straining a groin or pulling a hamstring right out of the box. So we'll just start with the basics – numbers every Brewers fan should know something about.

No point in sweating bullets over these questions. If you don't know these then you don't deserve to make the final cut for the Opening Day roster.

Question 1: What Brewer went homer-less in 1,762 at-bats from 1987 until 1991?

Question 2: What pitcher did the Brewers pay $6,750,000 for his 1-3 record in 1993 and his 1-5 record in 1994?

Question 3: Who played 15 seasons for the Brewers, collecting 2,281 hits in 1,856 games?

Question 4: For whom did the Brewers retire the number 19?

Question 5: On August 19, 1995, Wisconsin Governor Tommy Thompson, Milwaukee County Executive Tony Ament, Milwaukee Mayor John Norquist, and Brewers President Bud Selig revealed a financial plan for a new stadium worth what amount?

a) $200 million
b) $250 million
c) $300 million
d) $350 million

Question 6: What 19-year-old rookie sensation made his Major League debut with the Brewers in 1988? He moved from third base to shortstop to replace an injured Dale Sveum and his first Major League hit was a home run.

a) Pat Listach
b) Ernest Riles
c) Gary Sheffield
d) Greg Vaughn

Question 7: What Brewer, despite playing in the minor leagues until late May, won the 2007 National League Rookie of the Year award with a .324 batting average and 34 home runs and 97 RBI in only 113 games?

a) Ryan Braun
b) Prince Fielder
c) Corey Hart
d) Rickie Weeks

Question 8: In 1978, this Brewers rookie hit .273 in 125 games and placed second behind the Tigers Lou Whitaker in Rookie of the Year balloting.

a) Paul Molitor
b) Cecil Cooper
c) Robin Yount
d) Gorman Thomas

Question 9: In 2006, this Brewer led National League rookies with 28 home runs.

a) Ryan Braun
b) Prince Fielder
c) Corey Hart
d) Rickie Weeks

Question 10: Name the rookie phenom who was the third pick overall in the 1973 Major League Baseball draft. (Hall of Famer Dave Winfield was the fourth pick that year.) This Brewer made his Major League debut in April of 1974 and was only 18 years old.

    a)   Don Money

    b)   Cecil Cooper

    c)   George Scott

    d)   Robin Yount

Question 11: This former Brewer finished his Hall of Fame career with 755 home runs.

Question 12: What Brewers legend had his number 4 retired and went by the nickname "The Ignitor"?

Question 13: What Milwaukee icon was inducted into the Baseball Hall of Fame with a career batting average of .200 and 14 career home runs?

Question 14: Name the famous trio of teammates who compiled a Major League record 6,399 hits during their playing years together.

Question 15: This legend played all of his Major League seasons with the Milwaukee Brewers. When Brewers President Allen H. (Bud) Selig signed him to a three-year contract after this player's 1989 MVP season, he stated, "There is a whole generation of people who grew up watching [him] play for the Brewers. That fact was not lost upon me or a lot of other people. I received a wonderful letter from a teacher in Madison who said the same thing to me. She said that she had grown up watching [him]. She couldn't imagine the Brewers or herself not having that privilege as long as he played. In my mind and my heart, this is what it's all about." Name this legend.

Question 16: On April 28, 2001, this Brewer crushed three home runs to help Ben Sheets record his first Major League victory.

    a)   Jeffrey Hammonds

    b)   Geoff Jenkins

    c)   Jose Hernandez

    d)   Richie Sexson

Question 17: What Brewers slugger surpassed Willie Mays as the youngest player ever to hit 50 home runs in a season?

Question 18: What Brewers slugger won a 2009 Louisville Slugger's "Silver Slugger Award." These awards are given to the top hitters at each position in the American and National Leagues according to a vote by Major League coaches and managers.

a) Ryan Braun
b) Mike Cameron
c) Prince Fielder
d) Casey McGehee

Question 19: Who was the first player to record 3,000 hits for the Milwaukee Brewers?

Question 20: Who holds the Brewers single season RBI record?

a) Ryan Braun
b) Cecil Cooper
c) Prince Fielder
d) Gorman Thomas

Question 21: This Brewers pitcher finished with 324 career wins. However, he only recorded 26 of those wins with Milwaukee. Name this pitching legend.

a) Rollie Fingers
b) Eddie Mathews
c) Warren Spahn
d) Don Sutton

Question 22: Who holds the Brewers record for most strikeouts in one season with 264?

a) Mike Caldwell
b) CC Sabathia
c) Ben Sheets
d) Don Sutton

Question 23: What season did the Brewers pitching staff toss a franchise record 31 consecutive scoreless innings?

a) 1978
b) 1981
c) 1987

d) 1990

Question 24: What Brewer became the first Mexican-born pitcher to win 20 games in a season in the American League?
a) Rickey Bones
b) Teddy Higuera
c) Juan Nieves
d) Jamie Navarro

Question 25: What pitching legend recorded 37 saves for the 2009 Brewers?

Question 26: What manager led the team known as "Bambi's Bombers"?

Question 27: What former Oakland A's manager was hired to manage the Brewers beginning with the 2009 season?
a) Ken Macha
b) Rene Lachemann
c) Davey Lopes
d) Dave Stewart

Question 28: In 2005, the Selig family turned over the Brewers to this Los Angeles financial wizard.
a) Mark Attanasio
b) Warren Buffet
c) Bill Gates
d) Donald Trump

Question 29: After the Brewers exciting 2005 season, considered by some to be their best season since 1992, the organization announced that it would extend a three-year contract to what executive?
a) Mark Attanasio
b) Harry Dalton
c) Doug Melvin
d) Wendy Selig-Prieb

Question 30: What Brewers skipper earned his 500th win on August 26, 1998, against the Colorado Rockies? He is the only Brewers manager to accomplish this feat.

Question 31: On June 25, 2005, these two Brewer rookies slugged their first Major League home runs in the same game.
- a) Prince Fielder and Corey Hart
- b) Prince Fielder and Rickie Weeks
- c) Rickie Weeks and JJ Hardy
- d) Rickie Weeks and Corey Hart

Question 32: In 2009, this Brewer led the National League in hits with 203.
- a) Ryan Braun
- b) Prince Fielder
- c) Bill Hall
- d) JJ Hardy

Question 33: Juan Nieves became the first Brewer to throw a no-hitter. He also became the first Puerto Rican-born pitcher to throw a no-hitter in the Major Leagues. What year did Nieves accomplish this feat?
- a) 1986
- b) 1987
- c) 1988
- d) 1989

Question 34: Three times the Milwaukee Brewers have had four representatives in the All-Star Game. The last year they accomplished this feat was 2007. Which player was *not* one of the 2007 All-Stars?
- a) Prince Fielder
- b) Bill Hall
- c) JJ Hardy
- d) Francisco Cordero
- e) Ben Sheets

Question 35: What Brewer holds the franchise record of 18 strikeouts in one game?
- a) Moose Haas
- b) Teddy Higuera
- c) Ben Sheets
- d) Don Sutton

Question 36: Not since 1982 has a team captivated the city of Milwaukee like the 2008 Brewers. Prince Fielder, Ryan Braun, and CC Sabathia led this battling team into its first postseason in 26 years – making for a memorable season. The Brewers finished 90-72. What reigning American League Cy Young Award winner was traded to the Brewers on July 7, 2008, in a deal that General Manager Doug Melvin proved, "We're going for it!"

a) Roy Halladay
b) Cliff Lee
c) CC Sabathia
d) Johan Santana

Question 37: With only 12 games left in the season, Mark Attanasio's gutsy firing of manager Ned Yost proved to be a winning decision when this interim manager helped the Brewers win 7 of the last 12 games, clinching the Wild Card for the Brewers first postseason berth since 1982.

a) Ken Macha
b) Don Money
c) Dale Sveum
d) Cecil Cooper

Question 38: Who hit a walk-off two-run home run during a critical game against the Pittsburgh Pirates on September 23, 2008?

a) Ryan Braun
b) Prince Fielder
c) Bill Hall
d) JJ Hardy

Question 39: Who hit a walk-off grand slam during another must-win game against the Pittsburgh Pirates on September 25, 2008?

a) Ryan Braun
b) Prince Fielder
c) Bill Hall
d) JJ Hardy

Question 40: In the do-or-die 2008 regular season finale against the Chicago Cubs, what Brewer belted a go-ahead two-run home run in the eighth to lift the Brewers to a 3-1 win in front of 45,299 fans at Miller Park?

a) Ryan Braun
b) Prince Fielder

c) Bill Hall
d) JJ Hardy

Question 41: Who in the Brewers organization is known as "Mr. Baseball"?

Question 42: On June 12, 1997, the Milwaukee Brewers played their first interleague game and became the first American League team to play at this ballpark since the 1945 World Series.
a) Busch Stadium
b) Polo Grounds
c) Shea Stadium
d) Wrigley Field

Question 43: In 2001, this Brewer hit 45 home runs, tying Gorman Thomas's franchise record. He also came up one short of the Brewers RBI record of 126.
a) Carlos Lee
b) John Jaha
c) Geoff Jenkins
d) Richie Sexson

Question 44: What year did former home run king Hank Aaron return to Milwaukee as a Brewer? On April 11, Opening Day, Milwaukee declared "Welcome Home, Henry Day" and beat the Cleveland Indians 6-2.
a) 1973
b) 1974
c) 1975
d) 1976

Question 45: Name the Brewer who joined Hank Greenberg and Stan Musial as the only players to win the MVP award at two different positions.

1 SPRING TRAINING ANSWER KEY

1. Jim Gantner.

2. Teddy Higuera. If you are doing the math that comes out to $3, 375,000 per win.

3. Paul Molitor, 1978-92. His trade to the Blue Jays in 1993 devastated Milwaukee fans. Although fans missed this legend, they were happy to see him win a World Series with the Blue Jays. He finished his 21-year career with his hometown team, the Minnesota Twins. His 3,319 career hits is 9th all-time behind Pete Rose (4,256), Ty Cobb (4,191), Hank Aaron (3,771), Stan Musial (3,630), Tris Speaker (3,514), Carl Yastrzemski (3,419) Cap Anson (3,418) and Honus Wagner (3,415).

4. Robin Yount.

5. B – $250 million. On October 12, 1995, Governor Thompson signed the Stadium Bill into law in County Stadium's centerfield parking lot.

6. C – Gary Sheffield.

7. A – Ryan Braun.

8. A – Paul Molitor.

9. B – Prince Fielder.

10. D – Robin Yount.

11. Hank Aaron.

12. Paul Molitor.

13. Bob Uecker.

14. Jim Gantner, Paul Molitor, and Robin Yount.

15. Robin Yount.

16. B – Geoff Jenkins.

17. Prince Fielder. He hit 50 home runs in 2007 to set the Brewers single season home run record. His father Cecil Fielder hit 51 home runs for the Detroit Tigers in 1990. They are currently the only father/son duo to each hit 50 home runs in a season.

18. A – Ryan Braun.

19. Robin Yount.

20. C – Prince Fielder, with 141. In 2009, Fielder broke Cecil Cooper's record of 126 RBI in a game against the Houston Astros. Interestingly, Cooper, serving as the Houston Astros manager, witnessed Fielder's feat from the visitor's dugout at Miller Park. Cooper and Fielder's paths had previously crossed when Cooper managed in the Brewers minor league system while Fielder was working his way up to the Big Leagues.

21. D – Don Sutton.

22. C – Ben Sheets.

23. D – 1990.

24. B – Teddy Higuera.

25. Trevor Hoffman. He completed 2009 with a Major League record 591 career saves.

26. George Bamberger.

27. A – Ken Macha.

28. A – Mark Attanasio.

29. C – Doug Melvin.

30. Phil Garner.

31. B – Prince Fielder and Rickie Weeks.

32. A – Ryan Braun.

33. B – 1987.

34. B – Bill Hall.

35. C – Ben Sheets.

36. C – CC Sabathia.

37. C – Dale Sveum.

38. B – Prince Fielder.

39. A – Ryan Braun.

40. A – Ryan Braun.

41. Bob Uecker.

42. D – Wrigley Field.

43. D – Richie Sexson.

44. C – 1975.

45. Robin Yount – shortstop in 1982, centerfield in 1989.

"[Paul] Molitor didn't walk across the lake to get here and he didn't change his clothes in the phone booth. He's just a tough hitter."

— *Doc Edwards*

2 OPENING DAY

They all count now, no pressure. You made the roster with the big club and now you're looking forward to earning a seven-figure contract, some major endorsements perhaps, or being a part of the Sunday Conversation on SportsCenter, but most importantly, you're here to help the team earn a chance to play in the playoffs. So game on, let's find out how well you can perform in the clutch after we toss some 95 MPH fastballs your way while mixing in some nasty sliders. The categories stay the same, but the questions are now big league caliber. We're about to find out whether or not you can play this game for a living.

Question 46: What attendance milestone have the Brewers achieved in 2008 and 2009?

Question 47: In 1987, Paul Molitor captivated Major League Baseball with his hitting streak. How many consecutive games did he hit safely in?

Question 48: Who did the Brewers select as the first pick in the 1985 Major League Baseball draft?

Question 49: In 1991, this Brewer hit .325 (fourth best in the American League) with 216 hits and 133 runs scored. Most impressively, he hit .388 with two outs. Although his individual statistics were some of the best of his career, he was quoted as saying, "It's always difficult to talk about a year when things have gone well personally, but when you've been disappointed by what's happened collectively ... The season was a disappointment because as a team we ended up watching baseball in October rather than playing. We were frustrated by another year gone by and another lost opportunity of getting back to the World Series" (Brewers.com). Name this player who was selected as the Brewers 1991 team MVP.

Question 50: Robin Yount holds the Brewers record for most runs scored. How many runs did he score during his 20-year career with Milwaukee?
   a) 1,264
   b) 1,386
   c) 1,593
   d) 1,632

Question 51: In 1985, this Brewers pitcher was named *The Sporting News* Rookie Pitcher of the Year and finished second for the American League Rookie of the Year award. Name this pitcher.
   a) Teddy Higuera
   b) Jamie Navarro
   c) Juan Nieves
   d) Dan Plesac

Question 52: In 1999, this pitcher was the Brewers first round draft pick (tenth overall). In 2000, he pitched for the United States National Olympic Team in Sydney, Australia and tossed a complete game shutout in the Gold Medal Game against Cuba. In 2001, he finished 11-10 in his Major League rookie season. Who was this pitcher?
   a) Jeff D'Amico
   b) Doug Davis
   c) Julio Machado
   d) Ben Sheets

Question 53: In 2009, this Brewer hit .301 with 16 home runs and finished fifth in the National League Rookie of the Year Award voting.
   a) Alcides Escobar
   b) Mat Gamel
   c) Jody Gerut
   d) Casey McGehee

Question 54: What Brewers rookie broke Oakland A's slugger Mark McGwire's record for highest slugging percentage (.618) for a rookie?
   a) Ryan Braun

b) Prince Fielder
c) Geoff Jenkins
d) Greg Vaughn

Question 55: Who became the first Brewer to hit a home run in his first Major League game?
a) Geoff Jenkins
b) Paul Molitor
c) Gary Sheffield
d) Greg Vaughn

Question 56: What Brewer became the first player to have two four-hit games in a single World Series?

Question 57: In addition to his home run prowess, this Brewers legend was known for his tailgating with fans before and after the games. He hit 175 home runs for the Brewers from 1978 to 1982, including 45 homers in 1979. Name this legend.

Question 58: Ned Yost, a former teammate of this Brewers legend, stated in an MLB.com article, "I was drawn by his passion, his love of the game, his energy, the way that he played the game with an all-out style. He was a guy that I could really relate to. I tried to play the game as hard as he did." Who is this Brewers legend that went by the nickname "Gumby"?
a) Jim Gantner
b) Charlie Moore
c) Gorman Thomas
d) Pete Vuckovich

Question 59: Considered to be one of the founding fathers of relief pitchers, this Brewers legend ended his career with a record 341 saves. (Note: The all-time save record has since been broken multiple times.) Name this pitcher.

Question 60: Who is the first player to be inducted into the Hall of Fame wearing a Brewers hat?

Question 61: What Brewer set a franchise record with 53 doubles in 2004?
a) Jeff Cirillo
b) Geoff Jenkins
c) Lyle Overbay
d) Richie Sexson

Question 62: Who holds the Brewers record for highest season batting average of .353?
a) Ryan Braun
b) Jeff Cirillo
c) Paul Molitor
d) Robin Yount

Question 63: On May 21, 2003, what Brewer hit three home runs in the same game for the second time in his career?
a) Jeromy Burnitz
b) John Jaha
c) Geoff Jenkins
d) Dave Nilsson

Question 64: On May 21, 2005, this Brewer recorded his 1,000th career RBI, helping Doug Davis notch a 6-0 shutout against the Minnesota Twins.
a) Jeff Cirillo
b) Bill Hall
c) Carlos Lee
d) Geoff Jenkins

Question 65: What two Brewer teammates combined for 389 hits in 1989?

Question 66: In 1993, this player became the first pitcher in Brewers history to lead the league in innings pitched with 258.
a) Cal Eldred
b) Graeme Lloyd
c) Jamie Navarro
d) Bill Wegman

Question 67: Who holds the franchise record for most shutouts in one season with six?
a) Mike Caldwell
b) CC Sabathia
c) Ben Sheets
d) Jim Slaton

Question 68: In 1985, this Brewer became the first visiting pitcher to throw a one-hitter at Yankee Stadium in 17 years.
a) Moose Haas
b) Pete Ladd

    c) Pete Vuckovich
    d) Bill Wegman

Question 69: Who pitched the Brewers past the Chicago Cubs in a critical 2008 season finale 3-1 win? After the Brewers win and a Florida Marlins win over the New York Mets, the team clinched its first postseason berth in 26 years.
    a) Dave Bush
    b) Yovanni Gallardo
    c) CC Sabathia
    d) Jeff Suppan

Question 70: What two Brewers each threw a scoreless inning in the 2004 All-Star Game at the Houston Astros' Minute Maid Park?
    a) Ben Sheets and Dan Kolb
    b) Ben Sheets and Chris Capuano
    c) Dan Kolb and Chris Capuano
    d) Ben Sheets and Doug Davis

Question 71: In 1978, this Brewers manager earned *The Sporting News* Manager of the Year award.

Question 72: What Brewers manager helped coach in the 2005 All-Star Game?

Question 73: What Brewers manager owned the tavern Cesar's Inn on 56th Street and National Avenue, a relay throw's distance from County Stadium?
    a) George Bamberger
    b) Harvey Kuenn
    c) Buck Rodgers
    d) George Webb

Question 74: Who replaced Harvey Kuenn as manager after the club's 87-75 record in 1983?
    a) George Bamberger
    b) Alex Grammas
    c) Rene Lachemann
    d) Tom Trebelhorn

Question 75: Mark Attanasio's first big move as Brewers owner was to sign this player to a four-year $38.5 million deal in 2005.

a) Ryan Braun
b) Prince Fielder
c) Eric Gagne
d) Ben Sheets

Question 76: Robin Yount won American League MVP awards in 1982 and 1989. Who is the only other Brewer to win an MVP award?
a) Cecil Cooper
b) Prince Fielder
c) Rollie Fingers
d) Paul Molitor

Question 77: On May 10, 2001, this Brewer crushed three home runs at Miller Park to help lift the Brew Crew to an 11-1 win over the Chicago Cubs.
a) Jeromy Burnitz
b) Jeffrey Hammonds
c) Geoff Jenkins
d) Richie Sexson

Question 78: In 2004, this Brewer recorded 70 stolen bases.
a) Corey Hart
b) Scott Podsednik
c) Junior Spivey
d) Fernando Vina

Question 79: Right before the 1990 All-Star break, the Brewers pounded the California Angels 20-7. Darryl Hamilton hit his first career grand slam. How many runs did the Brewers score in the fifth inning?
a) 8
b) 11
c) 13
d) 17

Question 80: On July 31, 1990, Nolan Ryan became the 20th pitcher to win 300 games when he defeated the Brewers 11-3 at County Stadium in front of 51,533 fans. Who was the losing pitcher that day for Milwaukee? He gave up five earned runs in 5.1 innings pitched.
a) Chris Bosio
b) Teddy Higuera
c) Jamie Navarro

d) Bill Wegman

Question 81: There is no more celebrated Brewers squad than the 1982 team that lost to the St Louis Cardinals in Game 7 of the World Series. On June 1, 1982, this manager took over the Brewers on an interim basis. The Brewers were 23-24 and seven games out of first place in the Eastern Division, tied for fifth place. This manager inspired the Brewers to win 72 of their next 115 games to finish the season with a Major League best 95-67 record. Name this celebrated Brewers skipper.

Question 82: In June of 1982, the Brewers won 20 of 27 games. They also set an American League record for most home runs in 15 consecutive games. How many home runs did "Harvey's Wallbangers" crush during this 15-game stretch?
   a) 20
   b) 25
   c) 30
   d) 35

Question 83: By how many games did the Brewers win the Eastern Division title?
   a) 1
   b) 2
   c) 3
   d) 5

Question 84: On October 3, 1982, what Brewers pitcher picked up the win to clinch the Eastern Division title?
   a) Mike Caldwell
   b) Jim Slaton
   c) Don Sutton
   d) Pete Vuckovich

Question 85: True or False: The Brewers were down 0-2 to the California Angels and became only the second team in history to overcome an 0-2 deficit to win the American League Championship Series.

Question 86: In 2006, this Brewers team MVP hit 35 home runs and collected 85 RBI.
   a) Prince Fielder
   b) Geoff Jenkins

c) Bill Hall
d) Carlos Lee

Question 87: On September 29, 2000, the Milwaukee Brewers played their last game at County Stadium in front of 56,354 fans. The 100-minute closing ceremonies were led by Bob Uecker and included appearances by Hall of Famers Hank Aaron and Warren Spahn of the Milwaukee Braves, Rollie Fingers and Robin Yount of the Milwaukee Brewers, and Jim Taylor and Willie Davis of the Green Bay Packers. To whom did the Brewers lose their final County Stadium game to 8-1?
a) Chicago Cubs
b) St. Louis Cardinals
c) Cincinnati Reds
d) Chicago White Sox

Question 88: Who is the Brewer remembered for both his long ball and league-leading strikeouts? In 1987, he became the first player in Major League history to have 100 more strikeouts than RBI (186 strikeouts to 80 RBI).

Question 89: In what year did the Brewers find themselves in an exciting pennant race only to have their postseason dreams come crashing down when the Toronto Blue Jays clinched the American League Eastern Division on the second to last day of the season?
a) 1989
b) 1990
c) 1991
d) 1992

Question 90: What Brewer holds the franchise record for most stolen bases with 412?
a) Sixto Lezcano
b) Paul Molitor
c) Fernando Vina
d) Robin Yount

2 OPENING DAY ANSWER KEY

46. They went over the 3,000,000 mark!

47. 39 – only six players in the history of Major League Baseball have had longer streaks. Joe DiMaggio of the New York Yankees (56 games in 1941), Willie Keeler of the Baltimore Orioles (45 and 44 in 1896-97), Pete Rose of the Cincinnati Reds (44 in 1978), Bill Dahlen of the Chicago Colts (42 in 1894), George Sisler of the St. Louis Browns (41 in 1922), and Ty Cobb of the Detroit Tigers (40 in 1911).

48. BJ Surhoff. The Brewers passed on Will Clark (San Francisco Giants), Barry Larkin (Cincinnati Reds), Barry Bonds (Pittsburgh Pirates), Rafael Palmeiro (Chicago Cubs), Randy Johnson (Montreal Expos), David Justice (Atlanta Braves), John Smoltz (Detroit Tigers), and Mark Grace (Chicago Cubs).

49. Paul Molitor.

50. D – 1,632.

51. A – Teddy Higuera.

52. D – Ben Sheets.

53. D – Casey McGehee.

54. A – Ryan Braun (.634).

55. A – Geoff Jenkins – in his Major League debut on April 24, 1998, Jenkins hit a home run against the Giants Orel Hershiser.

56. Robin Yount.

57. Stormin' Gorman Thomas.

58. A – Jim Gantner.

59. Rollie Fingers.

60. Robin Yount.

61. C – Lyle "Ooooooooo" Overbay.

62. C – Paul Molitor, 1987.

63. C – Geoff Jenkins.

64. C – Carlos Lee.

65. Robin Yount and Paul Molitor.

66. A – Cal Eldred.

67. A – Mike Caldwell.

68. A – Moose Haas.

69. C – CC Sabathia.

70. A – Ben Sheets and Dan Kolb.

71. George Bamberger.

72. Ned Yost.

73. B – Harvey Kuenn.

74. C – Rene Lachemann.

75. D – Ben Sheets.

76. C – Rollie Fingers.

77. A – Jeromy Burnitz.

78. B – Scott Podsednik.

79. C – 13.

80. A – Chris Bosio.

81. Harvey Kuenn. Five days after the Brewers lost Game 7 to the Cardinals, Brewers General Manager Harry Dalton dropped the word

"interim" from Kuenn's title. In a November 1982 What's Brewing article, Dalton said, "We think it is fitting that Harvey returns to manage the Brewers in 1983. He played a major role in the Milwaukee Brewers' finest season ever, leading them to the American League Championship and a near miss in the seventh game of a World Series. He was just what the doctor ordered." The article went on to report that the reason it took five days before the Brewers announced Kuenn's appointment for the next season was the organization's concern with his health. This courageous manager had overcome heart problems, stomach surgery and a leg amputation.

82. D – 35.

83. A – 1.

84. C – Don Sutton.

85. False – the Brewers became the first team to overcome an 0-2 deficit to win the American League Championship Series.

86. C – Bill Hall.

87. C – Cincinnati Reds.

88. Rob Deer. Deer also had 100 more strikeouts than RBI during his 1991 and 1993 seasons with the Detroit Tigers. With 186 strikeouts in 1987, Deer set a league record that was eventually passed by Jack Cust in 2008. Deer is the easiest person to strikeout in Major League history, averaging a strikeout every 2.56 at-bats. His .220 career batting average is one of the lowest of all-time. On a positive note, Deer's patience and large presence at the plate resulted in many walks allowing him to have a respectable .324 career on-base percentage. He ended his career with 230 home runs.

89. D – 1992.

90. B – Paul Molitor.

54192100R00076

Made in the USA
Lexington, KY
05 August 2016